Confessions of a
Professional
Gummy Bear Giver Outer

BRANDON BOSWELL

iUniverse, Inc.
New York   Bloomington

Confessions of a Professional Gummy Bear Giver Outer

Copyright © 2010 Brandon Boswell

iUniverse books may be ordered through booksellers or by contacting:

iUniverse
1663 Liberty Drive
Bloomington, IN 47403
www.iuniverse.com
1-800-Authors (1-800-288-4677)

ISBN: 978-1-4502-5004-7 (pbk)
ISBN: 978-1-4502-5005-4 (cloth)
ISBN: 978-1-4502-5006-1 (ebk)

Printed in the United States of America

iUniverse rev. date: 8/16/2010

For my Heavenly Father, my family, Ashley and Shelley

&

For Kim, Pam, and everyone at the
North Carolina Division of Services for the Blind

Contents

Chapter 1
When I was a child ...

LOOKING BACK ON MY CHILDHOOD (which thankfully hasn't been *that* many years ago) and thinking about the experiences I had growing up, I have come to realize many of my childhood memories are of events that really weren't all that life-changing. But when experiencing those events as a child, in my mind, they were nothing short of the end of the world.

There was that time in the third grade when, for music appreciation class, our teacher decided that the best way for us to better appreciate music was for us to learn how to play a musical instrument. In theory, that made sense, but the reality was that the instrument of choice turned out to be the recorder, one of the favorite choices among music teachers who suffer from hearing impairments.

It's my strong personal opinion that the recorder may very well be the most annoying musical instrument ever created. If I were to rate the pleasantness of the sound of a recorder, especially when played by a young child who is learning to play it, it would rank somewhere between the sound of a dentist's drill and fingernails on a blackboard.

It's also my opinion that the best way to interrogate captured prisoners of war is to bring groups of schoolchildren who are learning to play the recorder into the prison camps and force the suspected terrorists to listen to them perform the same songs over and over again until they finally crack and reveal all they know about plans for upcoming terrorist attacks. I believe doing this could potentially save millions of innocent lives.

Despite my belief that the recorder could be used as a tool for torture, our teacher liked the sound of it. We were assigned to learn to play one song on the recorder and perform in front of our families and friends. I'm pretty sure our families and friends were as reluctant to hear us play the recorder as we were about having to play the recorder in front of them.

The song we were assigned to learn was that musical classic, *Mary Had a Little Lamb*. I realize this sounds simple enough, and I will admit *Mary Had a Little Lamb* is probably far easier for a child to learn than say, *Flight of the Bumblebee*. But in the mind of an eight year old kid who had never played an instrument before and couldn't read a lick of music (and this is coming from a twenty-nine year old adult who still doesn't play an instrument and can't read a lick of music), this experience is nothing short of traumatizing. When faced with such a scenario, a child is likely to have visions of messing up so terribly on the recorder in front of his family and friends that his parents disown him and send him to live in an orphanage where he ends up chained to a stone wall and fighting off rats for his allotted one bowl of gruel per day. Sometimes the child envisions the worst possible outcome of them all where his parents allow him to stay at home, but he's sent to bed that night without dessert.

Faced with the possibility of such outcomes, I wasn't sure how I was going to handle this situation. I considered the possibility of waiting for the day of the recital and just simply letting the child next to me take the blame for my terrible recorder playing by saying it was them and not me who ruined the recital. Then I remembered most of my classmates had the ability to retaliate by getting me in a headlock and shaking me down for my milk money, and that was just the girls in my class.

Thankfully I was blessed with a family who came to my aide with love in their hearts (and probably cotton in their ears). My father tried his best to help me learn the notes of the song. He knows how to both read and play music, but he never really had the patience needed to teach music. To be more specific, he never had the patience to teach *me* music.

My father's instrument of choice in teaching me musical notes was the piano. However, at the end of an average lesson, which if I remember correctly was approximately ten minutes, it became apparent that my father had not raised a musical prodigy.

I must confess I can't remember all the details of our music lessons. I hadn't thought about this for a while, and some of the details are sketchy. I think this is due in part to our ability as adults to block out painful childhood memories as part of a coping mechanism. If I remember correctly, though, our music lessons often led to yelling, crying, and temper tantrums.

I didn't act much better myself.

(In later years, my father attempted to teach me to play

the piano by trying to teach me the notes to *Here Comes the Bride*. This led to nothing more than a tendency for me to cry at weddings for all the wrong reasons.)

We soon agreed that learning sheet music was something that didn't come naturally for me, but we also learned that I had a knack for memorizing sounds of music notes, and the order in which they were played. All I had to do was figure out which sound came after the next sound and simply memorize them long enough to perform in the recital. I realize I took the easy way out, but it's my belief that sometimes we're given an easy way out on purpose and to not take it as foolish.

The day of our program soon arrived. All of the parents gathered in the school auditorium for the musical program which included our lively rendition of *Mary Had a Little Lamb*. It was the first time I ever played a musical instrument in front of an audience. Coincidentally, it was also the last time I ever played a musical instrument in front of an audience. From start to finish it took less than one minute to perform. As quickly as it began, it was over. Amazingly I didn't mess up…too badly. Plus, I realized *Mary Had a Little Lamb* was far easier to play than *Flight of the Bumblebee*. It should be noted, though, that when you have a group of schoolchildren playing *Mary Had a Little Lamb*, or any song on instruments at the same time, it almost always sounds remarkably like *Flight of the Bumblebee*.

After that day, our teacher never had us perform again, which served as a great reminder that God does indeed hear the prayers of small children.

*   *   *

Looking back, my experience with the recorder is far

more laughable now than it was back then. This is true of many of my childhood events. Now that I'm an adult with a job, expenses, and the other responsibilities that come with adulthood, there's a part of me that longs for those simpler childhood days again, though perhaps not the musical parts.

It reminds me of that verse in I Corinthians (NIV) where the Apostle Paul says, "When I was a child, I talked like a child, I thought like a child, I reasoned like a child. When I became a man, I put childish ways behind me."

Had I been the one who had written that verse, I likely would have concluded it by saying, "But I did so with great reluctance and hesitation."

To be honest, I think some "childish things" are actually quite good, at least my childish things were.

I was a child of the Eighties and early Nineties (not the Fifties or early Sixties). Children then experienced many of the same problems we have today, but oftentimes in much smaller doses. Sometimes we were simply too young to realize there were any problems.

Growing up, I went to the birthday parties of friends and ate pizza, cake, and ice cream, and I can't recall ever being told about the dangers of watching your weight for fear of diabetes. I never worried about how many more calories I would have to burn off on the treadmill if I ate a second piece of pizza (or the third, fourth, or fifth piece, either). I drank sodas and never concerned myself with reading the nutritional level to see what the sugar content was in the drink.

It also seems it was much safer to eat certain foods when I was a child. These days, it seems like every other day some food item is being recalled for fear of contamination. When

I was a kid, a peanut butter and jelly sandwich was one of the greatest things you could eat. Now that same peanut butter and jelly sandwich could literally kill you.

I grew up playing with toys and nobody worried too much about if the paint on the toy was poisonous if ingested and could kill you. The group of kids I hung around with never really worried about reading the warning labels posted on toys because we were smart enough to know that a G.I. Joe action figure was meant to be played with and not swallowed whole.

We actually made it outside and ran around, maybe not as much as we should have, but almost certainly more than many children today. When we did play outdoors, sometimes we or someone we knew was fortunate enough to have some type of secret hideout in which to play, and if so, it was usually nothing as fancy as there is today.

It's my belief that the days of the children's tree house have come and gone. Today, the tree house has been replaced by overpriced clubhouses that come equipped with a kitchenette that includes a working oven and refrigerator, as well as a guest room for sleepovers, and extras like swings, slides, monkey bars, mini bars, and hot tubs. I've seen clubhouses that make me wonder if the children have to pay property tax to stay in there. These days, many toy catalogs look more like an issue of *Better Homes and Gardens*.

To put this in perspective, in my own neighborhood, it's been rumored that one particular children's clubhouse has wall-to-wall carpeting and cable television. When I was a kid, I had a cardboard box, the grass, and my imagination.

I suppose it doesn't really matter now anyway because these days, most children don't want to even leave their own homes. Many kids are perfectly content spending their free time sitting in front of their own fifty-inch, flat-screen television which has been mounted on the wall in their bedroom and watching some ridiculous TV show or making it to the next level of their newest video game.

Television. The days of *The Andy Griffith Show* and *My Three Sons* were long gone by the time I was growing up, and we were exposed to a considerable amount of sex and violence on the small screen. Compared to the shows of today, though, I really believe we were better off. During my childhood, a program that dealt with drug abuse, rape, and alcoholism was called a drama. Today, we deal with these same issues in sitcoms. Plus, I grew up in an era where we had never heard of reality television. 'Nuff said.

For a boy growing up in the Eighties who loved action adventure shows, we had great shows like *Simon & Simon*, *Airwolf*, *The Equalizer*, and perhaps my all-time favorite, *Magnum, P.I.* Not only did *Magnum, P.I.* have great storylines, but it was one of the first shows that featured main characters who had bravely served their country in the Vietnam War and depicted them in a positive light, and rightfully so. The show also taught me it was possible to go on an all-night stakeout while sitting in a bright red Ferrari and rarely be seen.

Though many today would argue that these shows were too violent, they did teach some valuable lessons. They taught that a gun in the hands of the wrong person could do great harm, but a gun in the hands of a good guy who knows how to handle a gun can prevent a lot of harm from ever happening in the first place.

Of course, not every action adventure show of this era promoted gun use. We had that show, *MacGyver*, which starred a character that was about as anti-gun as you could get. He could, however, make a homemade bomb out of battery acid, a pack of matches, a stopwatch, and a jelly doughnut, so I'm willing to overlook his views on gun control.

What about the video games? When I was a kid, we had video games, but our games were much simpler. The goal of our games was to save princesses while we dodged laser beams and fled from evil villains, as opposed to many of the video games of today where the goal is to mow down prostitutes while driving a stolen car and fleeing from the police. As much as technology has advanced in the last two decades, is this the best we can do?

When I was growing up, we didn't have anywhere near the level of technology available to us today, and yet, my peers and I turned out alright. Most parents would never have dreamed about giving their grade-school children a cell phone. Cell phones were much more expensive back then and weighed approximately thirty to forty pounds. Had some of the smaller, underweight children been given such phones, they would have found it too difficult to hold the phones while trying to remain standing upright.

Texting was unheard of during my childhood. If we wanted to communicate during class, we had to pass notes to one another without getting caught. Of course, this is wrong and just plain rude to the teacher, but rather fun for the students when we considered the possibility of the teacher intercepting the notes of some of our more-difficult-to-like classmates and reading them aloud to the whole class, thus revealing their latest crush of the week, and the hope (or fear) that we would be the object of the crush.

I grew up in the days before the words *Internet* and

e-mail were part of the English language. In the days before the Internet, when a student had to write a research report, they went to places called libraries and did research using these primitive things called books. The word *Wikipedia* had yet to be uttered in a sentence, let alone used as a reference in a report. People would have probably thought you were referring to some type of medical ailment (e.g., "Aunt Gladys has been suffering from chronic Wikipedia for years.")

If you wanted to get in touch with friends who lived far away, you would most likely have called them on a telephone, which was often connected to the wall with a cord. It was annoying, but it cut down on the chances of misplacing the phone since it's difficult to misplace a wall. For years, we didn't have the option of sending an e-mail, either. No, sir. Instead, we wrote a letter on a sheet of paper using a primitive writing tool called a pencil and sealed the paper in this thing called an envelope. On the upper right hand side of the envelope we practiced the ancient custom of putting this sticky object called a stamp on top. Then we walked outside (yes, you read correctly) and placed the letter in a mounted container on the house known as a mailbox. Then someone called a mailman would come, place our letter into a bag, and carry it off to this place called the post office. He would also leave other letters for us in the box. If we wanted to correspond with the letter writer, we had to repeat the same archaic process all over again. I truly believe that if you tried to teach some kids how to write a letter the old fashioned way, by the time they mastered it, they would be so excited they would actually e-mail their friends to let them know they would be sending them a letter.

Let me come back to the issue of guns for a moment. When I was growing up, there wasn't as much of a concern about kids playing with toy guns as there is today. A child could play with a toy gun and their parents were usually proud because they believed their child would grow up to be a police officer or serve in the military. In my hometown of Jacksonville, North Carolina, which is a rather large military community, I think some parents were actually more concerned when their children were not playing with guns.

Nowadays, because of school shootings and the media's coverage of such events, if a child is discovered playing with a toy gun, many parents will call in psychologists out of fear the child isn't well-adjusted.

Of course, you dare not bring a toy gun onto a school campus. If the gun is mistaken for the real thing, the school will go into lockdown and police officials, likely including the SWAT team, will be called to investigate and the child could face expulsion or even criminal charges.

Growing up, parents had more freedom in disciplining their children as well. There wasn't the level of fear that there is now about spanking a child. Recently I was watching a reality television program (for the record, I was bored out of my mind) in which every week a different family where the parents have little to no control over their children is spotlighted. The children commonly act like this show is just a warm-up for all the on-screen work they know they'll be doing when they're older and being shown kicking and screaming in the backseat of a police car on an episode of *Cops*.

After it's shown just how unruly the child is (or children are), the next step is to bring in a professional nanny to help get the family back on track. The concept of this type of program isn't the worst I've ever seen, but what I don't like about these types of shows is that I don't ever recall seeing any episode where the parents are encouraged to spank their children when it becomes necessary. The worst punishment I ever saw was having the child spend time in something called "the reflection room." While in the reflection room, the child's punishment is usually something like spending time alone thinking about what horrible and unspeakable act they committed. The number of minutes (not hours) they spend in there is determined by how old the child is. If the child is five years old they would spend five minutes in the reflection room. I guess that means that if a family has a nine year old who decides to hotwire the family minivan and go joyriding around the neighborhood, if that child is caught, that child faces the fear of having to spend nine whole minutes in the reflection room thinking about what they did.

Just like the children's tree houses, it's my belief that gone are the days of the old fashioned "wood shed" that so many children could greatly benefit from visiting with their parents from time to time. These days, if a child thinks he'll get spanked, he'll threaten his parents by pulling out the cell phone they bought for him for his fifth birthday and inform them that if they lay a hand on him, he'll call Social Services, whose number has already been pre-programmed into the phone by the child.

*   *   *

In the retail store where I work, I see children and teenagers of all shapes and sizes and backgrounds. When I see these young people who are being trained to be our leaders of tomorrow, I think about the demands and pressures our culture has placed on them as well as their parents who have the responsibility of raising them during this most important and difficult time in their lives.

Like everyone else, I have my own opinions on the subject of parenting. Not being a parent myself, I'm probably the last person in the world who needs to give parenting advice, but anyone who knows me well knows that not having any previous knowledge on a subject has never stopped me from being an expert on it.

There are many beliefs about child rearing in the 21st century that just absolutely annoy me. For example, we have children being taught that EVERYBODY is a winner and there are no losers. Let me clarify by using the following example:

Two children are competing in a school track and field competition. They're both lined up at the starting line and the coach shoots the starting pistol. (Actually, it's likely that the coach will use a CD with the recorded sound of a starter pistol since having a starter pistol on the school campus would be in direct violation of the school's zero tolerance policy, so I should say that coach hits the play button on the CD player and the race begins.)

After a hard-fought race, one child crosses the finish line before the other. Now in theory, the child who finished first is the winner and should be acknowledged for winning, assuming he did so fairly. The child that crossed the finish line second is the loser in the race, but assuming he tried his best, he should still be acknowledged for his effort as well.

The problem is that many in our culture want to take

away the concept of losing for fear that if a child does lose, the loss will damage their self-esteem.

In the case of the child losing the race, the "leading experts" would fear this loss will be the negative turning point in the child's life that leads him to become emotionally scarred and develop a deep depression where he loses all interest in sports and school. Eventually he'll drop out of school, become a drug addict, will be unable to hold down a steady job, have an emotional breakdown, go on a five state murder spree, and land in jail for life, or three years with good behavior, which ever comes first. Ironically, these events are usually closely followed by a book and Hollywood movie deal.

Here's the problem with this belief. If the losers are treated the same way as the winners, what incentives are there for the winners to keep trying their best and what incentives are there for the losers to work harder so they themselves can experience the joys of truly winning? A second place effort doesn't deserve a first place reward. This isn't an original statement, but it's one that bears repeating.

On the opposite end of the parenting issue, we have the other "leading experts" who believe young people must have tremendous amounts of pressure and stress placed on them so that they can successfully compete against their peers now and in the future. These are the ones who say it's either a first place finish or nothing at all.

Though I'm certainly for teaching our young people about the importance of hard work, there must be limits. Today, we have young girls starving themselves because they are told through the images they see in the media that if you don't look good enough, you're not good enough. We also have young boys being taught that if you don't drive the right automobile or have a job where you make a certain a mount of money, you're not good enough, either.

Here's my take, and though it's not a popular opinion in our culture, it's my sincere and firm belief that EVERYBODY is created by God in His image. He loves everyone equally, and ANYBODY, regardless of their G.P.A., business resume, financial portfolio, dress size, or muscle size, who allows God to work in their lives will have a life of true meaning and purpose. Why is it so difficult for us to learn this absolute truth when we're so willing to accept all the absurd lies?

*   *   *

Before I conclude this chapter, I want to share my opinion on one more belief about raising children today that just, as my Southern ancestors used to say, "Burns my biscuits."

Many parents have gotten the idea that the best way to show their children they're loved is to buy them thousands of dollars in overpriced toys, games, and electronics. They want their children to have all the things they didn't have as kids themselves. This child-centered approach, however, if not kept in check, can lead to self-centered children.

Don't get me wrong. I love getting gifts. Who in their right mind doesn't? But why must a parent spend their next paycheck on a gift that is likely to keep their child's attention for a few days (if that long) and in time is likely to be broken, lost, or completely disregarded by the child because he or she lost interest in the toy and has now turned their attention to playing with the cardboard box the toy came in?

The best gifts come from the heart, not the toy catalog. If you want to give a lasting present to a child, find out what the child likes to do and give them your time. For example, if the child likes animals, take a trip to a zoo where you and the child can enjoy watching God's creatures at work and play. If your child's interest is fishing, take the child on a fishing trip or even to an aquarium. Plus, for an added bonus, if we can get kids outdoors again, the obesity rates of American children will start to fall.

Parents, it's your choice: Make a memory...or make a credit card payment.

Also, despite what others may say, a handmade gift can be a great idea. Handmade gifts show your children or the children in your life how much you love them by showing them you found the time to make them something that came from the heart.

Through the years, many of my friends from college and graduate school have gotten married and now have children of their own. When I'm invited to their birthday parties, I want to have a gift for their children that shows how much I love them. After taking the time to get to know these terrific kids, I find out what they like, such as their favorite hobbies or cartoon characters. Then I go online to find pictures of those images, print them out, and sit down and draw a sketch for the child of their favorite things that I later have framed to give that child at the party. Through the years, I've done sketches from cars and trucks to various Disney characters. (Note: If any Disney lawyer happens to be reading this, please know I have NEVER taken one cent for any picture that I thought for one second is trademarked. I have been taught first and foremost to have a reverent fear of God, followed closely by a reverent fear of any lawyer affiliated with The Walt Disney Company.)

* * *

So, what can we take away from this rant on modern parenting? Simply this: Children and teenagers need to know that they are loved by their families and friends, and most importantly, by the God who created them. They need to be rewarded for positive behavior and punished for negative behavior. Plus, adults need to stops focusing on teaching these young people to be the best, but rather, to do the best they can.

When I meet a child or teenager, I often want to say to them, "Enjoy it while you can, kid. Once this part of your life is over, you can't get it back."

Today, we have children and teenagers taking piano, violin, trumpet, saxophone, flute, and clarinet lessons to give them a head start in competing for music scholarships and careers as professional musicians. They're also taking swimming, soccer, basketball, football, volleyball, cheerleading, and gymnastics lessons to give them a head start in competing for athletic scholarships and careers as professional athletes. Let's not forget the Spanish, French, and Latin lessons, along with multiple computer courses to give them a head start in competing for academic scholarships and high paying jobs in Fortune 500 corporations.

My question is, have we already taken their childhood away from them before it ever really began?

I will always believe children need the occasional spanking to keep them on the right path when they get off course. Maybe the same should be true for those adults raising these children as well.

Chapter 2
Yearbooks: The Needed GPS
for a Trip Down Memory Lane

IT'S MY OPINION THAT ONE of the greatest inventions to come along during my childhood was the creation of the Koosh Ball, or "rubber band ball," as it is called by many.

What made the Koosh Ball so much fun was that it came in a variety of colors and was fun to play with by yourself. Better yet, if you were trying to get a friend's attention, you could throw the ball directly at their heads without permanently injuring them.

Whenever I think of Koosh Balls, I think back to a day in high school when a friend brought a purple Koosh Ball to school and during our last break, he and I, along with some of our buddies, were standing around our classroom and talking while my friend was throwing the ball up in the air.

When he threw the ball up, it went a little too high and hit the ceiling but didn't come down. Instead, one of the rubber "strings" on the ball had gotten wedged in a tiny opening between two ceiling panels and hung there.

This may seem like a rather trivial event, but get a group of teenage guys together and the trivial soon becomes the extraordinary. A little Koosh Ball stuck on the ceiling and hanging by a string may seem like nothing to a group of teenage girls, but to a group of teenage guys, we felt like we had inadvertently created the eighth great wonder of the world.

As we all stood there staring up at the little Koosh Ball, we knew we were in the midst of something special. We were witnessing what we felt was a once-in-a-lifetime event, sort of like when you see the face of a dead President in a cheese Danish. We knew the chances of ever duplicating this throw so that the ball would get stuck again in that same tiny opening were one in a million, or about the same chances of getting through an entire family dinner without my mother reminding me that whatever I have in my mouth at the time, I need to chew it before swallowing it, and her believing me when I tell her that it's difficult to apply that rule when drinking milk.

Eventually the ball came down, but not before giving us a lasting memory we knew we would be sharing with our children and grandchildren in years to come.

The more I think about it, the more I believe my school days were similar to the experience with the Koosh Ball stuck in the ceiling panel. The problem was I felt like the Koosh Ball stuck in the ceiling panel.

Like the Koosh Ball, I often felt like I was being thrown up in the air, then back down, then back up again as high as possible only to get caught by a string, leaving me hanging in mid-air, and waiting to fall to the ground with those around not only anticipating my fall, but looking forward to it.

Looking back, I realize I never had a terrible school experience nor was I ever without friends, but with the daily pressures that came with school life, many good memories were overshadowed by the bad ones.

*   *   *

Shortly after birth, I was diagnosed as being legally blind, a diagnosis that has brought me both humility and humiliation throughout my life. My parents, who both worked in education, my father as a college professor and my mother as an assistant elementary school teacher, knew the cruelty that children can inflict upon their peers who are different from them. Many good children have suffered needlessly because of such childish behavior. Since I struggled because of my vision, my parents realized school would be difficult for me, both academically and socially.

From kindergarten all the way through high school, I always attended Christian schools in order for me to get the personal attention my parents knew I would need to succeed. Through the years, my parents paid a considerable amount of school tuition they could have spent just as easily on a down payment on a larger home or new cars, but they made the choice to put my needs ahead of their wants. To say I'm grateful for their sacrifice would be an understatement.

From kindergarten through second grade, I attended a rather large Christian school in Jacksonville. There is only so much about those early schooldays I remember. After looking through my yearbooks from that time, I was, however, reminded that my inability to look good in a yearbook photo occurred long before high school.

I was taught the basics, such as simple arithmetic: how

to add, subtract, multiply, and divide. I learned how to come up with answers to simple math problems without using a pocket calculator. With my math skills, however, I learned that I would need the calculator if I wanted to find the correct answer. I also learned the basics of good grammar and handwriting. I was never blessed with great handwriting, though. I'm convinced my teachers began analyzing my handwriting samples to see if I had any criminal tendencies.

I remember we also had a rest period as well, but it wasn't a nap time. Instead, we just laid our heads on our desks, which isn't as good as nap time. Even at that early age, I felt cheated. I believe all children should be allowed to have a nap time and there should be no age limits.

I also believe adults should be allowed a nap time in their daily jobs. An employer could make it part of their benefit package to include a cot, blanket, and pillow. Make it optional for at least thirty minutes. Many working adults could benefit from it and perhaps they wouldn't be so cranky so often if they were better rested. I know I have more than a few co-workers who could use a nap.

What I remember most from those early schooldays was that my principal, whom my family and I loved, left the school and was replaced with a new principal that many parents and students didn't like as much.

My parents decided to transfer me to another school several months before I entered the third grade. This proved to be a wise decision because so many parents were upset to see the old principal leave that they began pulling their kids out of the school themselves. By the following year, the school closed and was eventually torn down to make way for a drive-thru chicken restaurant.

I ended up transferring to a new Christian school that the former well-liked principal from my previous school helped to open. I had the honor of being one of the charter students, along with approximately thirty others.

In the early days of the school, money was tight and we were rather limited in resources. Today, the school continues in a beautiful, much larger facility, but back then, it was located in an old one-story office building that had seen better days. I later learned the school building was once used for an office supply store, a carpet store, and on two separate occasions, a cocktail lounge.

In the beginning, we didn't even have playground equipment. We were pretty limited in what activities we could do during recess. Sometimes we kicked balls at the school building or tried to see how long it would take to kick the ball onto the flat roof of the school. Then after we kicked the first ball on the roof, we realized we had to get it down, so then we kicked another ball on the roof to try to knock the first one down. We would repeat the process until we ran out of balls to kick. When we finally ran out of balls, some of the other boys and I would hang around in the alley between the school and the business next door. We were learning about the basics of juvenile delinquency and loitering at an early age.

This isn't to say we didn't have some exciting moments during recess as well. Since the school was located in a somewhat high crime area, many residents who owned homes in the neighborhood had large guard dogs chained up in their back yards that sometimes got loose and came onto the playground and tried to bite the students. When this happened, the teachers made us evacuate from the playground and get inside the school as quickly as possible.

We got very good at playing "Flee from the Rabid German Shepherd." After awhile, we were getting anxious to get playground equipment, such as a nice high-off-the-ground slide, if for no other reason to have something we could climb to get away from the neighborhood dogs and avoid the round of rabies vaccinations.

Within a few months, thanks to generous donations from the parents, we finally got playground equipment including a slide, swings, chin-up bars (which were fun to use for everything BUT chin-ups), and the personal favorite among the boys: the balancing beams.

During many recesses, the majority of the boys, me included, could be found on the balancing beams trying our best to maintain our balance while at the same time trying to throw one another off the beams by recreating some of the moves we learned from watching *American Gladiators*. This led to many occasions where the girls in our class got the chance to practice some of the moves they had learned from watching *Rescue 911*.

What I remember most about the school was that it was affiliated with a charismatic church. For those not familiar with the charismatic church, this is a denomination within the Christian faith that believes it's appropriate to hold a church service that includes a considerable amount of dancing and shouting during the service. Many of us in the Baptist church have a slightly different view. In my church, we believe it's not appropriate to dance during a church service. As far as shouting goes, we've been taught to only do that during church business meetings. There are other denominational differences as well between many Baptist churches and charismatic churches, including the differing views about the religious practice of speaking in tongues. Many charismatic churches believe it's permissible to speak in tongues during a worship service. In the Baptist church, we also believe it's permissible to speak in tongues, but only as long as it's not done out loud where anyone can hear you doing it.

I attended a church service there once, and the music was great and the sermon was outstanding. It was clear from the start that these were a group of faithful churchgoers who loved God and worshiped Him with all their hearts. Still, I couldn't get used to all the dancing and shouting during the service. As I watched everyone else, I kept wondering if this is what it was like during "Happy Hour" when this place used to be a cocktail lounge.

*   *   *

Shortly before entering the seventh grade, my parents transferred me to another Christian school in Jacksonville which had classes from kindergarten all the way through senior year. I spent six years at the school until my high school graduation in 1999.

Whenever I begin to get sentimental for those middle and high school days, I take out my yearbooks and begin flipping through the pages. I often go in order and look at the earliest pictures from the seventh grade and work my way up through senior year. One of the first pictures I always turn to is one of me standing beside a group of the most popular guys during a special chapel service on the first day of school. I must have said or done something to make them think I was cool enough to hang around with them. Apparently, it must have been a one-time thing because after that, it never happened again.

Thankfully, it wasn't long until I began making friends,

including my good friends, Alan, Allison, and her twin sister, Sheila. On the day I met them, I had broken my pair of glasses, and Alan walked over to where I was standing to make sure I was alright. Actually, at the time his father ran an optical shop and I think he was trying to make a sale on his behalf, but the sincerity was still there. Allison and Shelia also came over to make sure I was alright. Little did I know at the time that a pair of broken glasses would lead to my greatest life-long friendships.

The four of us soon began hanging out during breaks and our lunch period. There were two other girls in our group as well, which totaled four girls to two guys. Even then the odds still were not in my favor.

After our first year, one of the two other girls in our group moved away and the other remained but somehow managed to become popular. Since the rest of us hadn't reached the same level of popularity, she abandoned us for the cooler students. I remained friends with Alan, Allison, and Sheila, despite all the things that teenagers go through in middle school and high school that could have easily destroyed our friendship. We enjoyed the time we spent together and spent many breaks between classes and lunch periods together. On many Fridays in the fall, we could all be found attending school athletic events together as well. We all rode on the same bus to the football and volleyball games, but we were never able to sit together, though. Male and female students were not allowed to ride on the same seat together. Some days the girls rode in the front of the bus, while the guys rode in the back, and vice versa. We never had an official sex education class, but when it came to dealing with issues of sex and today's teenager, the school's basic policy was that as long as the male and female students have no contact whatsoever, nothing can go wrong.

Despite the bus rules, when we stopped to eat at a restaurant on our way home, Allison and Sheila were allowed to sit with Alan and me as long as we didn't sit on the same side of the booth. Many lasting memories were made from sitting together during those meals. Once our principal, Mr. Strickland, who was also our bus driver, drove us to a nearby town to have lunch at an all-you-can-eat buffet restaurant. As I was browsing through the buffet I saw what I thought was delicious chicken and pastry. I loaded up my plate and returned to my table, but as I took a bite, a very nasty taste entered my mouth. I quickly realized my chicken and pastry was actually white cabbage, apparently disguised as chicken and pastry to trick unsuspecting diners into eating it. The look on my face was priceless, and the laughter from Allison, Sheila, and everyone else was contagious. Even today, we still laugh and talk about the cabbage incident. This may seem like a meaningless experience to most, but to us, it's just one of the many memories that has made our friendship special.

These days, Alan serves in the military, and we haven't kept in touch like we should have, but I have kept in touch with Allison and Sheila. Through the years, we've grown to love one another for who we are. We learned to accept each other's faults and quirks and chose to find the good in the other. We chose friendship over popularity, and that's a choice I know none of us will ever regret.

*   *   *

The best way to describe my middle school and high school experiences is to say it was like being in a time warp.

It may have been the Nineties outside in the real world, but the second I walked through the school doors, it was like walking into what any American school would have been like back in the Fifties.

The school administration enforced a strict dress code which was carefully outlined in our school handbook. The boys were required to wear shirts with collars and long pants. If the pants had belt loops, then a belt was to be worn. If a boy forgot to wear a belt, it was rumored Mr. Strickland had made a belt for the boy to wear with the words "My Mommy Forgot to Dress Me This Morning" written on it. This accessory was certain not to improve any teenage boy's standing with any of the girls in his class.

Our hair wasn't allowed to touch our ears and sideburns couldn't go below the middle of our ear. This made it extremely difficult to ever achieve the "Elvis" look I wanted.

The girls were required to wear long dresses and skirts. Girls were NEVER to wear pants on campus. Apparently, there was a belief that girls who wore pants developed bad reputations.

We were taught from the King James Bible, and were warned to avoid tobacco products, alcohol, drugs, and rock music. Dancing was strictly prohibited, which was fine with me because on those few occasions that I attempted to dance, I looked like I had been drinking the same alcoholic beverages I was warned to avoid. We were also warned to avoid going to movie theaters, though on more than one occasion, I chose not to heed the warning.

During my junior year, I decided to rebel and go to a theater to see the movie, *Titanic*, which had just come out. I didn't tell anyone from school I was going to the movie out of a fear that one of my classmates might have ambitions of being an informant and would blow the whistle on me.

The night of the movie, I arrived at the theater with a friend who attended another local high school. We didn't hang around outside the theater any longer than necessary. I was afraid someone from school would see me walking into the theater and report me. For all I knew, school leaders were spying on me at that very moment, perhaps following me in an unmarked church bus with special windows so they could see me but I couldn't see them.

Later that evening as my friend and I watched the movie, I began to relax and enjoy myself, or at least I did until a certain memorable scene in the movie where Kate Winslet's character Rose asks Leonardo DeCaprio's character Jack to draw her wearing a rather expensive necklace…and only the necklace. Without going into too much detail, let's just say that during this particular scene Rose would have been in major violation of my school dress code. As far as what Jack was wearing at the time, I wasn't really paying attention.

As I watched this scene, I kept my eyes closed (most of the time) and prayed it would end quickly because of the fear that somehow word would get back to the school I had watched this and I would be expelled. I rationalized that if I couldn't see the sinful act, I couldn't enjoy the sinful act. This led to the mistaken belief that if you don't enjoy what you're doing, it isn't considered sinful.

*   *   *

Mr. Strickland was a man who had, and still has, a God-given love for children and teenagers and was one of the greatest principals any school could have. When I first arrived at the school, I admired the job he did so much I thought I'd like to be the principal of the school someday. When I told this to Mr. Strickland, he became very excited, but I wanted to make sure he knew I wasn't out to steal his job. I told him that I wouldn't take his job until he was dead first. It was around that same time he began to eat healthier and exercise more frequently.

Mr. Strickland always attempted to make our school experience as rewarding as possible, but it was clear that as long as he was in charge, our school would always have two things: prayer and a paddle. If a male student, regardless of age, was found to be in need of a good paddling, it would be given to him by Mr. Strickland free of charge to the student. If a female student was in need, Mr. Strickland's wife, who was in charge of the elementary students, was given the job. Neither Mr. nor Mrs. Strickland was ever accused of favoritism. They were equal opportunity paddlers. We knew they were serious, and during my time at the school, paddlings were few and to my knowledge we never once had a detention.

We knew we had it good, though. While many schools deal with such issues of drugs, guns, and teen pregnancy, a bad day for us was a student getting sent home early for being a flagrant gum chewer.

Rarely were there any fights. If there was one, it was usually just a couple of teenage boys involved in some friendly horseplay, or male bonding, as it is commonly called these days. Girls don't understand this because to them bonding involves hugging and crying. For guys, though, bonding involves headlocks, which is sort of like hugging. This can also lead to crying, too, now that I think about it.

I recall a series of incidents that occurred during a

couple of lunch periods during the winter of my freshmen year when one of the middle school students came to the misguided conclusion that he could beat any upperclassmen in a fight. He took it upon himself to provoke the older students into altercations, much to the delight of those of us in attendance.

When a teacher found out about the impromptu wrestling matches it became necessary to discontinue our daily lunchtime ritual. It's hard to explain why one student has another in a headlock. Since this was a church school, though, I believe we could have gotten away with it had we told the teacher we suspected the student in the headlock was demon-possessed and the other student who had him in the headlock was attempting to rid him of the unclean spirit, which made it necessary to cheer for the guy who had him in the headlock. Of course, any student cheering for the supposedly demon-possessed student would have had some serious explaining to do.

Mr. Strickland took his students' spirituality very seriously, and every Monday afternoon, he led school-wide chapel services where we were required to take notes from his sermons and later turn them in for a grade. He was an outstanding speaker who spoke of God's Word with great reverence. He talked about the importance of salvation, the rewards of Heaven, and the sorrows of an eternal Hell. Through his teachings I later came to ask Jesus Christ into my heart as we knelt together in his office one Tuesday morning when I was in the eighth grade.

Following chapel, Mrs. Strickland led rehearsals for the school choir, of which I was a member for six years. I was always a little afraid of Mrs. Strickland. She was a mother of five and in many ways was a mother figure to all the children under her care. She took that responsibility very seriously. While I was in choir, I went through that stage teenage boys go through where my voice began to change. As a result, sometimes certain sounds came out of my mouth similar to the sounds a wounded animal makes just before it's humanely "put down." Whenever this happened, Mrs. Strickland would publicly correct me by using her "mother voice," the voice that God gave to all mothers designed to strike fear in the hearts of children. She could say, "Brandon, you sang that last note too low," in such a way that it could make any teenage boy feel guilty that they hadn't been born a girl in order to remain a soprano for their entire life.

I will always have a special place in my heart for Mrs. Strickland, though. Even after many years, whenever I'm criticized publicly for singing off pitch, I still think of her with great fondness.

*   *   *

Next to spirituality, Mr. Strickland placed a major emphasis on academics. He wanted us to be the best students possible. We strove to maintain a strong work ethic, or at least maintain the appearance of one.

Our school used a self-taught curriculum where the students were taught math, English, and history out of booklets called PACEs. When a student completed twelve PACEs in a subject, it equaled one class credit. If we made anything below 80 percent on a PACE test, we failed and had to repeat the material. If we made 94 percent or above, not only did we pass, but we were given a piece of candy as a reward. This was of course a Baptist school, and as any devout Baptist will tell you, the reward of food is one of the best motivators for achieving success.

When a student failed, they were given a new copy of the PACE that had to be repeated which contained a little white slip of paper sticking out of the PACE with the student's failing score written on it. One of the worst feelings was taking a difficult test and waiting until the next day to find out if you passed or failed. This led to many restless nights for certain students, but also many great opportunities for practical jokes by their classmates.

My personal favorite was when a classmate passed a difficult test and another classmate made them think they had actually failed the test by cutting a white piece of paper the size of a failure slip and placing it into the PACE before the anxious test-taker arrived at school. Then the practical joker would watch from a safe distance at their friend's reaction to seeing the white piece of paper sticking out of their PACE and thinking they had failed. Granted, this was mean, but once we had to discontinue the wresting matches between the middle school and high school students, we had to fill the void somehow.

In addition to PACE work, we also had classes as electives, including Algebra I and Spanish I and II. Mr. Strickland's daughter taught Algebra I. Try as she might, she just couldn't get me to understand basic algebra. In fact, it became clear early on that many of my classmates were not blessed with great mathematical minds.

We never considered cheating on a test, though. This wasn't because of any deep rooted spiritual beliefs, but because we were afraid we might end up cheating off of someone who knew even less than we did and would receive an even lower grade. Thankfully, her grading scale was different than the PACE system. Any grade of 60 percent or higher was passing. The unofficial motto of the class quickly became "Solve for X, Pass with D."

Mr. Strickland's son-in-law was our Spanish instructor. He grew up in rural Minnesota, which isn't exactly a hub of Spanish-speaking activity. Thankfully, we used Spanish videos, and much of our learning came from the tapes. After graduating from high school, I never really continued learning the Spanish language. I took several Spanish classes in college, but they were beginner courses that just repeated what I had learned already in high school.

My Spanish teacher in college was never as much fun as Mr. Strickland's son-in-law. She was born and raised in South America. I always felt she set her expectations too high for her beginning Spanish students who she felt should master the Spanish language and speak it so eloquently by the end of their first semester they would be qualified to serve as the American ambassador to Venezuela.

After two years of Spanish classes in high school, we thought we were smart because we had learned to tell someone in Spanish that the burro is an animal from Mexico, which greatly aided us in engaging in meaningful conversation with the guy behind the counter at IHOT (the International House of Tacos) when we ordered a burrito combo. Since we were Baptist high school students, we were also expected to know how to say, "Repent for the end is near, sinner!" in Spanish as well, just in case the guy behind the counter at IHOT messed up our order and we had to take action. I also remember we learned the Spanish word for cheese is "queso," so now when I want to take a picture of someone, instead of saying, "Say, 'Cheese,'" I can say, "Say, 'Queso,'" instead, and sound much smarter.

In addition to the spiritual and academic condition of his students, Mr. Strickland was also concerned with our athletic condition, which in my case, left much to be desired.

All the students from the seventh grade upward were encouraged to take part in the school athletic program, which included flag football for the boys, volleyball for the girls, and both boys' and girls' basketball teams. Our school mascot was the eagle which came from our school verse in Isaiah where it states those that wait on the Lord will renew their strength, mount up with wings as eagles, will run and not grow weary, and walk and not faint.

Mr. Strickland was also our football coach, and he took competition very seriously. During any given practice, I did run and grow weary, and even when I walked I felt like fainting was always a distinct possibility. I was waiting on the Lord, but specifically I was waiting for Him to return to take me to Heaven so never again would I have to take part in another football practice.

Sports played a big role in the school, and the number of trophies our sports teams won through the years was quite remarkable for a school our size and those trophies were prominently displayed in a large trophy case in our school lobby.

When we had school-wide pep rallies, all the students as young as the first grade came to support our teams and watch our cheerleaders. The cheerleaders wore modest uniforms with skirts long enough that their knees were not visible to the human eye. In our school, a girl's knees were considered sacred, and to show them off in public was considered a scandalous act that would lead to nothing but shame for her and her family.

At the end of the pep rallies, the cheerleaders had a tradition of throwing small pieces of candy to the students. This led to another tradition of the high school students throwing themselves to the ground for a pack of Sweet Tarts while trying not to land on any of the first graders and inflicting bodily harm upon them.

Even though it was exciting to be a seventh grader on a football team, by the eighth grade I was opting for early retirement. I never made any really lasting contributions to the school's sports program, but I'm proud to say nobody ever carried a first aid kit as well as I did. Had I not graduated when I did it's almost a certainty I would have been promoted to water boy.

Because of my vision problems, I was never much of an athlete. I often felt that certain classmates looked down on me because I couldn't play the same games they played as well as they played them. I was often forced to sit on the sidelines, and not just at the sporting events. Sadly, even church schools can have social cliques, and there were days where I feared my time outside of class would be spent being teased or simply ignored by the other students.

The first trophy our school ever won was a Christian spirit award. As time went by, though, that trophy was quickly overshadowed by newer and larger ones from numerous football and basketball championships.

In I Samuel 16:7 (NIV) it says, "The Lord does not look at the things man looks at. Man looks at the outward appearance, but the Lord looks at the heart." I wish more people, especially teenagers, would take this verse to heart and get to know more of their classmates who may not throw a football or basketball as far or as high as they can, but make up for it with their other God-given talents.

As I looked through my yearbooks, I often paused to take a moment to look at the Dedication page in my tenth grade yearbook. That was the year the yearbook was dedicated to the memory of a former student named Thomas. Thomas had been a long-time student at the school and had moved two years earlier when his parents moved out of state. My first year at the school was Thomas' last year, and I didn't know him very well. The more I learned about Thomas later on, I realized I missed out on the opportunity to know a good and decent young man.

It was the night of the state football playoffs. Many Christian schools in our part of North Carolina played both boys' flag football and girls' volleyball in their own league. My school had won many championship playoff games over the years, but this playoff, however, would prove to one like no one had ever experienced.

The volleyball matches had concluded for the day, and all eyes were on the much anticipated championship football game the following day. On that cold, rainy night, reality reared its ugly head when word reached them about the death of Thomas. Their former classmate, who had been both an athlete and friend to many of them, had been killed in a traffic accident. Because I had not attended the playoffs that year, I wouldn't learn of the tragedy until the following week.

As my classmates were coming to terms with the death of their friend, Mr. Strickland knew the decision had to be made either to pack up and return home out of respect for Thomas or carry on with the task at hand of playing in the championship football game that was only hours away.

I don't know if a formal vote was taken, but the decision was made to stay and play in the championship game. I truly believe that is what Thomas would have wanted.

The following day, our football team played in the championship game. Months of intense training and practice had come down to this moment, and the end result was a victory, making our football team the winners of our state playoffs once more. The decision was made to dedicate their victory to Thomas.

The dedication concluded with the words of Psalms 116:15 (KJV): "Precious in the sight of the Lord is the death of his saints." It had taken a tragedy to remind us that life is short and no one knows when their time on this fragile Earth will end. Sometimes only a tragedy can put this in perspective.

*   *   *

As I continued looking through the yearbooks, eventually I would come to my senior yearbook. One of the first pages I turned to was my senior page. The senior classes were always small in number, including my own of only four graduates, and every senior had their own page in the yearbook where they wrote their final thoughts about their time at the school and what they hoped to accomplish in the years to come.

Often times, first and foremost, we thanked God for giving us salvation through Jesus Christ. We thanked our parents for the many sacrifices they made to send us to a Christian school, which technically was a private school. Mr. Strickland never wanted us to refer to it as such, though. He felt by telling others we went to a private school gave the impression we were too embarrassed to admit we attended a Christian school. I couldn't agree with him more.

We thanked Mr. Strickland, along with other teachers and school employees, who made our high school experience so special. Few teachers are given the credit they deserve for all the sacrifices they make to help educate their students, especially those that work in church schools. As little as our hardworking public school teachers are paid, many Christian school teachers work just as hard for far less pay and they would consider the annual salary of a public school teacher to be a major pay raise.

As I continued looking at the senior pictures, I was reminded how, when I first came to the school back in the seventh grade, some of the upperclassmen, including some of the seniors, took the time to speak to me and make me feel welcome, whereas other older students didn't seem to want to make the effort.

One upperclassman who always made me feel welcome was my friend, Abby, a beautiful blonde cheerleader to whom I had the honor of being briefly married, but not legally. Perhaps I should explain.

For a fun little experiment, Mr. Strickland decided to pair Abby and me off and we had to pretend to be a married couple and work together to prepare a meal. Our goal was to cook an egg over an open fire on the school grounds, using only the basics, which included one egg, matches, and pieces of wood and newspaper to use to cook the egg. Mr. Strickland put a time limit on us, which I believe was either five minutes or until the fire department showed up.

We struggled to make a fire, but somehow managed to cook the egg. The end result was Abby taking a spoon and force-feeding me the egg. My gag reflex kicked in and I ended up spitting the egg back out at her while some of it landed in her mouth.

The purpose of Mr. Strickland's experiment was to teach us about the cooperation that husbands and wives must have with one another if they want a successful marriage. To date, I'm still quite single, and I wonder if my experience with Abby and the egg had something to do with it. After seeing Abby in action, I realize that she took her role as "wife" very seriously. When the time comes for her to get married, I know she will make a wonderful wife. But if Abby's husband ever comes down the stairs one morning and says to her, "Honey, I'm late for work. Can you fix me some eggs really quick," may God have mercy on him.

*   *   *

Of course, when I look at some of those old yearbook photos, I don't always get the same sentimental feelings. When you attend a small school and you're not as popular or well-liked as the other students, you quickly become aware of it. Some of my classmates came from rich families, whereas I came from a family where both parents worked to pay my school tuition. Some drove nice cars, but my vision problems kept me from driving any car, nice or otherwise. Some also dated their most handsome or beautiful classmates, but regarding my dating life, I'll just say, "No comment."

Now that I'm older, I realize that many of my former classmates may not have been as well off as I thought they were. They had a lot of pressure placed on them to the best student or the athlete possible, get into the best college, get a high paying job, marry a handsome or beautiful spouse, and have numerous children who would follow in their footsteps. I'm certain such expectations caused them considerable turmoil, which perhaps led them to act the way they did at times. Many of my classmates went through some major struggles in their lives during and after high school.

I realize now that I may have been just as well off, if not better off, than the more popular students. I was never expected to be the best, which allowed me to make mistakes and learn from them. I wasn't expected to hang out with all the "right" people, which allowed me to become friends with many of the wonderful classmates that many other classmates never took the time to get to know.

It's been over eleven years since I graduated from high school. With the exception of Allison and Sheila, who are still my good friends, I've lost touch with most of my former classmates. Thanks to e-mail and social networking sites, I've kept in touch with a few classmates through the years, but Facebook just isn't the same as good-old-fashioned face-to-face contact.

Recently, I received a note via Facebook to inform me that several of my former classmates were planning a school reunion for anyone who ever attended our high school. It said in the note that they hoped to get the "old gang" together again. I was tempted to write back and ask if I was meant to receive the note about the reunion, because the way I remembered it, I never was really part of the "old gang." Had it not been for my friendship with Allison, Sheila, and Alan, high school would have been an even lonelier time for me.

Several weeks before the reunion, I e-mailed Allison telling her how I felt about seeing the "old gang." From the start, I never planned to attend the reunion, but out of respect for Allison and Sheila, I wanted to let them know ahead of time.

As I typed out the e-mail, I mentioned how much I loved her and Sheila, and that I did have wonderful memories of our school days. I also mentioned that some memories weren't so wonderful.

Allison wrote back and told me she felt the same way. She wrote how had it not been for Alan and me, along with a few other mutual friends, she never would have made it through on the friendship level. She said she was glad we had met those many years ago and how, had she never met me, she felt she would have been robbed of a blessing and a good friend.

I was reminded of the same thing.

The big difference between Allison and Sheila and me, however, was that they actually had the courage to attend the reunion. Allison mentioned in the e-mail that she didn't care about seeing some of the "old gang," but she was curious to see how some of our former classmates turned out. Her next words were priceless. She said that perhaps she was vindictive, but she wanted to rub some people's noses in what God helped her to accomplish in life.

Hell hath no fury like that of a Baptist woman scorned.

When I wrote her back, I made sure to tell her that if she decided to rub their noses in what God has helped her to accomplish that she should do it with the most Christlike attitude possible.

Shortly after the reunion, Allison e-mailed me to tell me how it went. The impression she gave me was that it was more like a Saturday outing. Most of our former classmates that for various reasons she hadn't been looking forward to seeing didn't even show up. Those that were our mutual friends did show up, and she and Sheila spent most of the reunion just talking and catching up with them.

In the first e-mail we had received about the reunion, it stated there would be an opportunity for any former students to speak about what they had been doing through the years. Neither Allison nor Sheila spoke about what they had been doing with their lives, but maybe that's for the best. Even though they had accomplished more than a few things worth bragging about, we had all learned a long time ago that in the end, it only matters what God thinks about how we live our lives, and not those around us who tend to focus on the superficial side of life.

*   *   *

To all the children and teenagers (and even adults) who are struggling to fit in at school or just in general, remember that many of the people you're trying to impress will be out of your life before you know it. If they don't like you for who you are, they're not worth having as friends.

This reminds me of a great line I once read in one of those annoying "send-to-all" e-mails I get far too frequently. It said in no uncertain words that the reason God allows some people to be a part of our past is because He never meant for them to be a part of our future. I had never looked at it that way before, but it makes sense.

Make an effort to be kind to the people who treat you badly. They may have serious issues in their lives of which you aren't aware, and you still need to deal with them with patience and understanding. If you're tempted to talk about them behind their back, do it in the form of a prayer asking

God to bless them and to help you to be a blessing to them. By doing so, you may even make a new friend.

Even if this doesn't happen, you can rest assured knowing that if you have God in your life, you already have the best friend you'll ever have. When you begin to feel like a Koosh Ball falling from a ceiling panel, you will know that God always will be there to catch you.

Chapter 3
When I Grow Up

"WHAT DO YOU WANT TO be when you grow up?" That is a question many kids are asked throughout their childhood. Most of the time they will quickly and enthusiastically spout off a list of dream jobs so long that any adult who dares ask the question had better not have any plans for the rest of the day if they want to hear the child's whole list.

When I was a kid, I spent a considerable amount of time wondering what my life would be like when I grew up. I spent countless hours daydreaming about all the really cool jobs I knew I would have and all the money I would make doing them, only to be brought back to reality by the gentle nudge of my schoolteachers who thought my time could be better spent elsewhere, like listening to them teach the lesson. How teachers can tell a child isn't paying attention, even though the child is staring directly at them, is beyond me.

Like all children, I had hopes and dreams of what I wanted to accomplish in life. Like many little boys, I wanted to grow up to become a police officer. To a young boy, a policeman has one of the coolest jobs in the world and from an early age I was taught to show respect for an officer of the law. In fact, at one point, my mother was on a career path to becoming a police officer, but my father was afraid it would be too dangerous. So instead, she opted to go into elementary education, which these days can be just as dangerous for a teacher in the classroom as it can be for the police on the streets. In some cases, teachers can deal with as many troublemakers as the police, but unlike the police, they can't be armed to defend themselves.

Many of the beliefs I had about law enforcement growing up came from all the images of police officers I saw on television, but I was too young to realize just how unrealistic such images really were.

Most TV cops were depicted as men who didn't take any nonsense from the bad guys and would do whatever it took to make an arrest. If a crime was committed, many times the officer happened to already be on the scene or was called to the scene with a response time of one minute or less. If the bad guy fled in a getaway car, which was usually a new Porsche or BMW, the officer would pursue him in his patrol car, which was either a standard black and white unit or, if it was a police detective in pursuit, it was usually a beat up, lime green sedan with smoke billowing out of the tail pipe. This would lead to a very cool but unrealistic police chase where, in order to catch the bad guy, the officer not only drove dangerously through city traffic, but also on sidewalks, through front lawns, and on rare occasions, through someone's house, in order to catch the bad guy and make the streets safer for all the good citizens who weren't rendered homeless during the pursuit.

Over the course of the pursuit, there was usually a series of near misses where either the bad guy or the officer came within inches of running down a group of small schoolchildren walking home from school, a group of old women walking home from their weekly Bingo game, or for a really dramatic effect, a group of wheelchair-bound nuns who were also blind and had seeing eye dogs tied to their wheelchairs that were leading them down the street.

During the chase, there was usually a considerable exchange of gun fire between the police officer and the bad guy. It wasn't uncommon for the bad guy to shoot out the windshield of the officer's patrol car. This made it easier for the officer to shoot out the back window of the bad guy's car. As the exchange of gunfire continued and since the officer's front windshield was already gone, this freed up the officer to continue shooting at the bad guy by spreading himself out on the hood of his police car and taking shots at the suspect while he continued to steer his patrol car through oncoming traffic by using his feet.

After the brief but destructive car chase covering either ten miles in one minute or the same mile ten times in one minute (and with a group of traumatized nuns to show for it), both the bad guy and the officer ended in a trash-filled alley where the lone cop cornered the suspect. It was usually the goal of the bad guy to get the officer alone in the alley all along because a gang of vicious hoodlums would be waiting to ambush the officer. However, most TV fight scenes which usually consisted of a handful of bad guys wearing ripped blue jeans, leather jackets, ski masks, and brandishing nun chucks, (and were as well-choreographed as any Shakespearian play I've ever seen) involved the thugs fighting the officer one at a time, as opposed to all of them joining in at once. This is somewhat similar to children waiting in a line to have a turn at the drinking fountain.

The officer, who was fully armed, would instead choose to beat up the bad guys one at a time using his martial arts moves which left each individual thug lying unconscious on the ground.

Five seconds after the last bad guy was lying on the ground, back-up would arrive. All the suspects would be brought to the station where the officer was already waiting for them after he had just finished his paperwork on the incident, which usually only took about five minutes to complete. This gave the officer enough time to go home to get ready for his date with his actress girlfriend that he loved with all his heart and wanted to spend the rest of his life with, even though after that episode, she was never seen again so they could make room for the next actress girlfriend that the officer loved with all of his heart and wanted to spend the rest of his life with as well.

Of course, scenes like this are totally unrealistic and don't do a good job showing the struggles police officers face on a daily basis in their personal and professional lives. I'm certain many men and women who entered careers in law enforcement because they were impressed by such images as children were in for a rude awakening on their first day at the police academy, which I hear isn't nearly as funny as those *Police Academy* movies make it out to be.

Plus, it seems these days that more people are cheering on the criminals than they are the police. Some known criminals are even given hero status, and the officers who risk their lives to protect those they are sworn to serve are viewed as villains in the eyes of those in their community.

I get so tired of watching news coverage of the mothers of known criminals stand in front of a camera and say, "My son would NEVER have done these things. He's a good boy and wouldn't hurt anyone. He's a regular churchgoer who knows all the commandments by heart."

Apparently, her son must have thought that the commandments on not killing and stealing were optional.

Just once before I breathe my last breath, I want to see the mother of a known killer go on TV and say, "My son is guilty as sin. I have failed as a parent, and my child has failed as a human being. I want everyone to know that if he is sentenced to death by the electric chair, I will be more than happy to pull the switch myself. If he ever gets out of jail, when I get my hands on him, he's gonna wish he had gotten sentenced to death in the electric chair."

Now **that's** good parenting.

In my case of wanting to be a police officer, it didn't matter, though. Because of my vision problems, it wasn't possible. It's just as well because it's safer when you can see what you're shooting at, though likely not as much fun.

Plus, I've never been the greatest judge of character. When I watched police shows and tried to figure out who the bad guy was out of all the possible suspects, I was wrong most of the time. Had I become a police officer, and we didn't have such things as DNA testing, it's likely there would be a considerable number of innocent people sitting on death row right now. It's for similar reasons why I didn't become a lawyer, either.

Like many children, I also wanted to become a doctor, but that dream lasted only about ten seconds. Even though I would love to make the money some doctors make, I hate germs and don't enjoy being around sick people, which is usually a prerequisite for being a doctor.

Don't get me wrong. I believe physical contact with others is very important. A life without human touch and compassion isn't a life worth living, but some human touch I can clearly do without.

For example, I HATE shaking hands and have no use for this practice whatsoever. When I encounter someone for the first time, I want to be polite, but not by shaking hands. For all I know, they could have just come from cleaning out a septic tank, and frankly, I don't want to find out.

What's worse is feeling obligated to shake hands with people you've known for years but they act like it's the first time you've ever met and they insist you shake your hand EVERY single time you meet. After awhile I want to say, "Look, we've known each other for over ten years. We've established a relationship and since we're already close friends, I see no reason why we should feel obligated to have any physical contact with each other ever again."

Why can't we just wave or bow at each other and leave it at that?

My views on kissing are slightly different. I believe kissing falls under the heading of "good human touch," assuming the human touching you doesn't creep you out. Of course, it's very possible to get sick as a result of the germs you're exposed to when kissing someone. However, if you kiss someone you love and end up in a hospital bed with a fever of 104 degrees, chills, nausea, and you keep seeing bright lights above you and hearing dead relatives beckoning you to "come home," you can take comfort in knowing it was all worth it.

Of course, sometimes kissing can fall under the heading of "bad human touch," and this actually did affect my career path. For years, I wanted to be a professional game show host and thought people like Bob Barker had the coolest job in the world hosting *The Price is Right*. My outlook changed as I grew older and began to notice all the contestants Bob dealt with on the show, which I believe fell into three categories, "Attractive College Co-eds," "Military Heroes," and "Everyone Else."

I think it's safe to assume Bob probably had no problems letting the attractive college co-eds kiss him. As far as the military heroes went, my view is since these folks are willing to risk their lives for their country, they had every right to kiss Bob whether he liked it or not. I did, however, feel sorry for Bob when he was kissed by "Everyone Else," who in my opinion were some of the scariest people to ever walk this Earth. There were times I could sense the fear Bob had when these contestants came up on stage and began shaking his hand and slobbering all over his face. After I watched his now famous fight scene with Adam Sandler in *Happy Gilmore*, I wondered if Bob ever had to fight the temptation to recreate that scene when these types of contestants came on stage.

There were other jobs on television that I thought about doing, such as being the host for a travel show. When I was a kid, I wanted to travel the world, but since I couldn't see very well, I knew I'd be an international incident waiting to happen. Plus, there are so many dangers in traveling abroad these days. I'm the type of person that could go on a luxury cruise only to have the ship struck by an iceberg and my only source of rescue would be a ship of sea pirates who happen to be infected by a new strain of influenza found previously in only pigeons and Labrador Retrievers.

One of my biggest childhood dreams was growing up to be a famous artist. Once my parents gave me a paint set as a Christmas present and I drew a lake scene with trees and a small house that was as good as any five year old could draw. The problem was, I was twenty-three when I drew it.

I have drawn since childhood, mostly with pen and paper, which has worked for me much better than paint. I took a few art lessons as a child, but I had to discontinue the lessons because money was very tight for my parents at the time. I learned a lot from those lessons, though, such as how to draw better trees and angles on buildings. I'm proud to say God has blessed me with the ability to draw great cars, houses, buildings, trees, and pretty much any basic landscape scene.

Drawing cars has been my favorite, though. When as a kid I could draw the most lifelike car crashes. I think this stems from the influence of yet another one of my favorite childhood police shows, *CHiPs*. In almost every episode, Ponch and Jon would attempt to stop someone for a routine traffic violation, and this would result in yet another car chase where a patch of L.A. freeway quickly became a demolition derby with a variety of two-ton Buicks and Ford sedans flying through the air. This was made possible by the jump ramps that were conveniently located on the freeway before the accident. Most of the cars would eventually end up landing in the back of a loaded oil tanker or a truck carrying fireworks. Amazingly, even after many of the numerous explosions, most accident victims just walked away.

What I wasn't blessed with, however, was the ability to draw people, especially human faces. Most faces I drew looked like they were the victims of the car accidents on *CHiPs* who weren't so fortunate.

Once I decided to draw a sketch as a birthday present for the young daughter of friends and made the terrible mistake of attempting to draw the Disney Princesses. After I was done, it looked like Sleeping Beauty had just gotten out of bed ten minutes ago and Snow White had gotten into a fist fight with all seven dwarfs. Even worse, Jasmine and Cinderella looked like they had gotten into a catfight to see who would be the first to dance with Prince Charming at the ball. Thankfully, Prince Charming was easier to draw since all I had to do was stand in front of a mirror and draw exactly what I saw, minus the glasses, receding hairline, and slight pot belly.

As bad as I am with drawing people, I'm even worse with animals. Once I drew a sketch of Cinderella's horse-drawn pumpkin carriage, and the horses looked like whatever kind of animal you get if you crossbreed the Loch Ness Monster with a wiener dog.

*   *   *

Of course, when you're a child, your parents, teachers, and friends will have their own thoughts about what they want you to accomplish with your life. Sometimes their dreams and your dreams won't always be the same.

For years people have told me I should become a pastor. It's statements like these that make me realize these people apparently don't know me as well as they think they do.

One reason why I never wanted to become a pastor is because some congregations expect way too much from their pastors. Of course, the members of a church have the right to expect their pastor to teach God's Word faithfully and to show love and concern for those in need. Some churches, however, expect their pastor to be a "Spiritual Superman" and they set very unrealistic expectations. A pastor can easily get himself into trouble if the members of his church expect him to do a hundred different things and be in a hundred different places all at once. I don't think it's necessarily wrong to want your pastor to be with you in the hospital if you're having a kidney transplant, but I do think it's wrong to insist the pastor donate one of his kidneys for the operation.

*   *   *

Though I never had any real desire to become a pastor, throughout my life I've served my church in various ways, and the pastors that I worked with over the years have taught me many valuable lessons.

I don't believe, however, that I could ever deal with all of the issues that a pastor has to face on a daily basis, such as preparing for upcoming church services. No matter how hard a pastor tries to ensure that everything in the service goes smoothly, sooner or later, mishaps will occur that are beyond the pastor's control. These are the same mishaps that often prove to be a great source of amusement for those sitting in the congregation.

There was the time in my church when an elderly deacon named Frank got up to pray just before the ushers passed the collection plates. Halfway through the prayer as he was attempting to say, "And help us remember God loves a cheerful giver," Frank got a little tongue-tied and instead said, "And help us to remember God loves a joyful sinner."

This was perhaps one of the few times in modern church history a pastor was praying he wouldn't hear an "Amen" shouted in a church service. I don't recall if the church collected any extra money that week, but weekly attendance did seem to increase from that point.

In another series of incidents years earlier, a former pastor had to deal with our church sound system that, for whatever reason, picked up on the frequency of CB radios of truckers driving past the church. When this happened, whatever the trucker was saying on his CB was broadcast over the loud speakers in the sanctuary for everyone sitting in church to hear. I'm certain our pastor was afraid the day would come when he would be standing behind the pulpit delivering a sermon on the dangers of temptation and as he shouted, "When the Devil tries to tempt you to do wrong, brothers and sisters, what will you say?" Just then, over the loud speakers, we would hear, "That's a big 10-4, good buddy." This scenario also falls into the "hope you don't hear an 'amen'" category as well.

These days, our current pastor faces problems involving the overhead screens in the sanctuary not working properly during the church service. During the singing of the hymns, when the words of the hymns are supposed to be shown on the screens, sometimes the computer system acts up and the words don't appear on the screens at the right time, if at all.

Now, it's not that we don't have hymnbooks. We do, and members of the congregation could just as easily pick them up from the rack in front of them and start singing. The mindset of some church members, though, is that the church paid thousands of dollars to install these overhead screens so they wouldn't have to use the hymnbooks. Picking up the hymnbook and turning to the correct page and singing the correct song is simply too much work and defeats the whole purpose of spending all that money on the screens that flash the words in front of them so they can avoid such unnecessary toil and labor. When the screens don't work properly, this leaves some in the congregation not singing at all. If they do sing, some are likely to just make the words up as they go along. Hymns such as *Here Am I, Send Me* may become *Hear They Are, Send Them* and the chorus to *Just a Closer Walk with Thee*, may end up being sung:

Just a closer walk with me,
"Come on, baby," that's my plea.
Then she turned and she maced me.
"Leave me be," she said. "Leave me be."

Perhaps the only hymn where the words are rarely messed with is *Onward, Christian Soldiers*. For many of us in the Baptist church, the lyrics to this hymn are sacred. The words "Onward, Christian soldiers, marching as to war …" help us to mentally prepare ourselves for upcoming church committee meetings.

Of course, some problems pastors face during a church service are their own doing. For instance, early on, every pastor learns when they have an altar call, it's important to turn off their lapel microphone as soon as somebody walks down the aisle to speak to them. If the microphone is left on, part of the conversation between the pastor and the other person will be broadcast for the whole church to hear. I imagine it would be unnerving if one of the most beloved elders of a church walks to the altar to speak to the pastor, and moments later the pastor is heard over a loud speaker saying, "You've been a drug addicted, alcoholic, Nazi sympathizer for HOW long??!!"

*　　　　　*　　　　　*

As if dealing with faulty sound equipment during a

church service isn't bad enough, sometimes pastors also have to interact with church members during the service, too. Many pastors quickly discover some of these same church members are a little "faulty" themselves.

When a pastor is standing behind the pulpit reading the morning announcements, after he's finished, he knows he'll have to ask the question, "Have I left anything out?" This is one of the most dangerous questions any pastor can ask because they face the risk of having a dozen church members raise their hands at once to inform the congregation what announcements were left out. Often times, the church members who feel led to speak are the ones who are known to have a great love of the sound of their own voice, and nobody else shares that love. These people can take a twenty second announcement and turn it into a ten minute monologue. They may have even been practicing what they were going to say at home that morning in their mirror (the one with all the mysterious cracks in it).

It's one thing if someone wants to inform the church that it's the church's week to volunteer at the local soup kitchen. It's another thing altogether when that person stands there rambling on about the time they served at the soup kitchen and made a point to speak to an elderly woman who sat alone in the back of the soup kitchen eating her meal who, unbeknownst to the talkative church member, was actually sitting in the back hoping that church member wouldn't notice her so she could avoid having to talk to someone who doesn't know how to shut up.

After the person has finished talking (and everyone else in the congregation has begun to regain consciousness), the pastor thinks the whole ordeal is over. At that point, though, that same long-winded church member, who appears to be getting ready to sit down, stands straight up again and says the three words no one ever wants to hear during a church service: "While I'm up..." This is usually followed by the next five words no one wants to hear during a church service: "Can I talk briefly about...?" Regular churchgoers know from experience that when certain people say they are going to talk briefly about something, it's rarely brief. Certain people have no grasp of the concept of "briefly," including some pastors, too. When certain pastors begin their sermons on Sunday morning by saying, "Today, I want to talk briefly about...," this is a signal to the congregation letting them know that if they want to sit down to lunch before 1 p.m. they will have to discreetly use their cell phones to place a takeout order and have the food delivered to the sanctuary so they won't miss the last thirty minutes of the sermon. Some pastors may not take the hint if they see church members staring at their watches, but when the pastor notices the ushers passing the collection plate to raise money to tip the pizza delivery boy, they usually know by this point that it's time to call it a day.

Another time pastors get nervous interacting with the congregation during a church service is during responsive readings. The concept of the responsive reading is quite simple. The pastor reads a line out loud followed by the congregation reading the next line out loud. However, some congregations have never fully mastered the responsive reading. Some pastors realize their church will never speak the same words together in unison. At best they might be able to do it in rounds.

When doing responsive readings, pastors must be on guard. For example, a pastor knows that when doing the responsive reading about the role of the virtuous woman, when he gets to the point in the reading where he says, "She will do him good and not evil all the days of her life," if any of the married men in the congregation give their wife a dirty look after that line, the pastor knows he may end up breaking up a fight.

It's for such reasons why I don't think many pastors attempt to do such readings any more than necessary, especially the ones dealing with unity in the church. This is a concept many of us in the Baptist church have yet to fully grasp. In some Baptist churches, if a pastor dares to do a responsive reading about unity it's likely this is how it will end up:

Pastor: "How good and pleasant it is when brothers live together in unity!"
Congregation: "You're fired, pastor!"

*   *   *

Perhaps nothing strikes terror in the heart of a pastor more than having to give up his allotted time behind the pulpit on Sunday to someone else when the church holds a special worship service that calls for guest speakers.

If the pastor selects the speaker himself, he will try to find just the right person to come and preach a respectable sermon, which leaves him free to enjoy a much needed Sunday off.

If the pastor doesn't have a say in who is chosen, however, this can make the pastor nervous. If the selected speaker turns out to be really bad, the pastor fears he'll still get blamed. If the speaker is really good, the pastor may worry the congregation will like the guest speaker more than they like him and they'll ask him to resign so the guest speaker can become their new pastor. Whatever the outcome, I'm certain some pastors fear that certain guest speakers, regardless of how good or how bad they are, may end up costing them their ministerial career.

In the Baptist church I attend, we have both a Baptist Men's Sunday and Baptist Women's Sunday where men and women, usually members of the congregation, speak on what being a Baptist man or woman means to them. They share what their lives were like before they were Christians and how Jesus Christ changed their lives for the better. Many times these speakers are well-spoken and sincere. After hearing them speak, I can feel God at work among the congregation.

This, however, is not always the case. There was the time during Baptist Men's Sunday where one of the guest speakers, a long-time member of the congregation, spoke to everyone about what it was like for him growing up with an abusive parent. He then proceeded to talk about an incident where he barricaded himself in his family home with a shotgun waiting for that parent to arrive. Knowing that certain members of the congregation, particularly the elderly, would not feel comfortable hearing this, he reassured everyone that he had no intention of killing the parent, but simply just shooting his knee caps out from underneath him.

The best way to describe some of the Baptist Women's Sundays I've attended is to say it's probably similar to what it's like sitting in the audience during an *Oprah* taping. Instead of the ushers passing the collection plates, they should have passed out Kleenex to help ensure everyone would make it through the service. In all seriousness, many of the women in the congregation have opened up about some private and very painful moments in their lives, and I greatly admire them for having the courage to do so. I will say, though, had Dr. Phil chosen a different career path and ended up going into the ministry and becoming the pastor of my church, he would never have had a dull moment.

At the conclusion of such services, usually the pastor will stand before the congregation and say something like, "Now, let's all thank our deacons for organizing such a wonderful service." This can be translated, "Don't blame me. I had nothing to do with any of this. Blame the deacons."

*   *   *

While I'm on the subject of the roles of the pastor in the church, I feel I should get a little more in-depth about something I mentioned earlier: the altar call. To me, the altar call is the most exciting and dramatic portion of the church service. As the congregation sings the final hymn, the pastor stands before everyone to give them an opportunity to make a public decision for the Lord. Whether it's salvation through Jesus Christ, joining the church, or just simply praying at the altar, this part of the church service can be the most exciting for the pastor, and also the most frustrating.

When the preacher invites members of the congregation to come and pray at the altar, most people who feel led to do so will leave their seat, quietly walk down the aisle during the singing of the hymn, kneel at the altar, and pray for whatever God has laid on their heart. When they have finished they quietly walk back to their seat. I view this as a sincere and humble act of worship to God.

It's my belief, however, that sometimes, certain individuals who pray at the altar during a church service are doing it just for show. Only God knows their heart, and it's not my place to judge, but I'm certain quite a few pastors down through the years have noticed the way certain members of their congregation act inside the church and outside of church. When the two behaviors are compared, drastic differences are noticed.

If I were a pastor, I would insist that two specific items be located at the altar. The first item is a kneeling bench where sincere churchgoers could pray more comfortably and it's easier for them to get up and down. The next item I would have is a trap door directly below the kneeling bench that can be released with the push of a button and only I would have access to the button. That way, insincere church members would think twice about putting on a show for the congregation when they should be more concerned about their own relationship with God.

I believe trap doors would also make church business meetings move along much quicker. If you have heads of church committees who always take too long behind the microphone, just make them stand on top of the trap door and place a time limit on them. The second they go over that limit, just release the door, and wait for the applause from everyone else.

*　　　　*　　　　*

Perhaps the greatest pastor I have ever known was Dr. Murphy, who faithfully served my church for over ten years. He was always there for my entire family. When my mother suffered a major heart attack and was transferred to a hospital more than fifty miles from our home so she could have surgery, Dr. Murphy drove those fifty miles on a cold winter's evening through the rain and wind to be with us.

A year later, when she was diagnosed with cancer, he came to our home to help us through the first shock that comes when a family member is diagnosed with such a terrible illness. I remember he read aloud from his Bible, though I can't remember what specific Scripture passage he read. I believe the verses were part of the Psalms. I was more impressed with Dr. Murphy's simple act of compassion of reading those encouraging verses to us.

It was Dr. Murphy who also first encouraged me to get involved with church outreach visitation. By encouragement, I mean one Sunday night he stood before the church and said, "Brandon, come out and help with visitation." A good pastor knows from years of experience that a little guilt can go a long way when it comes to filling vacant church positions.

For the next year, I went with Dr. Murphy on Monday night visitation. Every week we carried a stack of visitation cards with names and addresses of people to visit. Dr. Murphy was determined to visit EVERY single one of those people even if it killed us. On some occasions it almost did. There were times we found ourselves in certain neighborhoods that even the criminals tried to avoid. To protect myself, I carried a cell phone for two reasons. The first was that if we had to call 911, we would have the phone handy. The second reason was the phone I carried was one of the older cell phones that weighed between thirty to forty pounds and was roughly the same size as a small human head. If we were attacked, the phone was large enough to be used as a blunt weapon.

Fear of imminent death never stopped Dr. Murphy, though. He was persistent. Even in the worst neighborhoods, he was determined to find the right house. If he didn't find the right house, he usually found some house and was willing to visit whoever lived there. Dr. Murphy was so focused on meeting new people and encouraging them to join the church that he was often completely oblivious to any dangerous activity around us. I'm convinced that if the day ever came where we ended up walking into a trailer being used as a meth lab at the exact moment the meth was being cooked in a dirty, roach infested kitchen by a group of toothless, drugged-out hillbillies, Dr. Murphy would approach the druggies, offer them a handshake and a smile, and the first words out of his mouth would be, "I hope I'm not interrupting your supper." If the sheriff's department happened to raid the trailer while we were there, Dr. Murphy would likely say, "I'm sorry, I didn't know y'all had company coming over." Later, as the druggies are being led to the back of a patrol car, Dr. Murphy would likely be following behind, giving the deputies church brochures and offering the druggies his business card in case they need a job reference when they get out of jail.

I know this scenario sounds like a stretch, but Dr. Murphy is the same pastor who, when the relative of a church member opened up a candy store in our area, stood behind the pulpit and encouraged the congregation to shop in the store, which ironically was named "Sinfully Delicious." I'm sure Dr. Murphy wasn't the first Baptist preacher to promote a business with the word "Delicious" in its name, but he may be one of the few to ever promote a business with the word "Sinfully" in the same name.

*   *   *

Like many pastors, Dr. Murphy also took on the role of peacemaker in the church from time to time. I can tell you from firsthand experience that conflicts between church members can arise very quickly. On many occasions, pastors deal with members of their church coming to them and informing the pastor that another member of the church stole their property. This usually means somebody "stole" their favorite space in the church parking lot or their favorite pew in the sanctuary. When such allegations occur, a good pastor knows he must intervene quickly. Otherwise, families will be divided, blood will be spilt, or worse, cars will be towed.

A seasoned pastor knows *anything* has the potential to lead to conflict in the church, especially gossip. It seems like in many churches there is at least one small group who feel it's their responsibility to find out every little tidbit of information about everyone else in the church and share that information with anyone who will listen. These are the same people that stand in the choir on Sunday morning and sing *I Love to Tell the Story*, and you know they really do. If they can't find anything to gossip about, then they simply make it up as they go along.

If, for example, the church holds a bazaar and one of the elderly women in the church is kind enough to bake her "world famous" homemade fudge to sell, all it takes to stir up trouble is for someone else in the church to remark, "You know, I don't believe that Miss Ethel's fudge is homemade. It tastes like store-bought fudge." When situations like this occur, any smart pastor knows it's time to prepare for what may be the mother of all battles.

Once word gets out concerning the allegations made about Miss Ethel's fudge, or "Fudgegate," as it will likely be called, church members are likely to begin taking sides, especially the elderly ladies in the church who are closest to Miss Ethel. (I can say from personal experience that the older women in my church have always scared me. When I hear the term "The Church Ladies," I place it in the same category as I would "The Bloods" and "The Crips.")

Miss Ethel, being a founding member of "The Church Ladies," is likely to become so outraged about the allegation that she tried passing off store-bought fudge as "the real thing," that she will threaten to leave the church, and will also encourage all her friends to leave with her in an act of unity. It will turn out that many of them are more than willing to do so. It may take the pastor days, and perhaps even weeks, to smooth this situation over. Even if the pastor can somehow restore peace in the church once more, he knows he's walking a thin line. If he does something stupid like showing Miss Ethel how much he appreciates everything she does for the church by buying her a box of store-bought fudge as a gift, Miss Ethel is most likely to respond by saying, "And just what exactly are you implying, young man??!!"

And the battle rages on.

My own church has been no stranger to conflicts, either. Once the members of the church were having a lively debate (and by that I mean an all-out holy war) on what style of worship service we should have: a traditional worship service with hymns, piano and organ music or contemporary worship with drums, guitars, and praise music. Without mentioning which side I took, I'll just say that I wasn't always on the winning side, but yet, I was never wrong.

We finally voted on this latest pressing issue at the monthly business meeting. Before we voted, Dr. Murphy attempted to bring unity in the church by standing before us and telling what I like to call "The Purple Church Story." This is the story that many pastors tell during times of vital decision making in their church about a group of church members who come together to vote on what color to paint the sanctuary and it's decide to paint it purple. Though the ones who wanted to paint it a different color are upset, they accept the vote and even help to paint the sanctuary purple. I've heard this story more than once, and I'm convinced it's one of the first things future ministers learn as first-year seminary students in *Peacemaking 101*.

"The Purple Church Story" has always annoyed me. It always ends at the point where everyone accepts the decision to paint the sanctuary purple. It never goes on to mention what happens after the sanctuary is painted purple. What happens if visitors come to the church for the first time and are so freaked out by the purple paint job they never come back and even encourage their friends to never visit the church in the first place?

I don't believe I could ever focus on worshiping God in a church with purple walls. I would keep wondering why anyone in their right mind would paint the sanctuary to match the skin tone of Barney the Dinosaur. In some churches, the members are likely to take sides when the decision to paint the sanctuary is between the colors of white and off-white.

*   *   *

After ten years of preaching, witnessing, spiritual advising, peacemaking, and occasional refereeing, Dr. Murphy retired from my church. His influence on my life continued as I later served in the church as a deacon.

I was ordained as a deacon during a Sunday evening

church service in late September. During the ordination, I knelt down in the front of the sanctuary while the other deacons walked up, placed their hands on my head, and prayed that God would bless me and my service to the church. At the same time I was praying that every deacon who laid their hands on my head had remembered to wash them after they went to the restroom before the service. Laying your hands on somebody's head also falls into my category of "bad human touch."

In my three years as a deacon, I maintained regular contact with my assigned deacon families, was never involved in any scandalous love triangle with any church members, and nobody tried to impeach me. By accomplishing these things, I actually accomplished more than some of the previous deacons in my church.

I've never read any books about what it takes to be a good deacon, nor could I say for sure just how many books there are on the topic. I will, however, mention what I learned as a deacon that should be shared.

I learned it's important for deacons to maintain contact with the church families that are assigned to them. This could include sending a birthday card or get well card to a church member, or perhaps even arranging to have a meal sent to them if they were too sick to cook. Many church members, especially the elderly and shut-ins, usually appreciate these little gestures. A deacon (or anyone else, for that matter) should never underestimate what a simple act of kindness can mean for someone who feels lonely or left out.

One of the most humbling experiences I ever had as a deacon was when I sent a letter to an older lady in my church to simply inform her that I would be serving as her deacon. I later found out that in all the years she had been in our church, I was the first deacon ever assigned to her that took the time to contact her. That comment touched me in a way she'll never know.

When I first became a deacon, I wasn't a big fan of sending cards to anybody. This is due in part to an experience I had back in high school. Shortly before graduation, I sent out graduation invitations and many recipients responded by sending me gifts, usually a check for the amount of twenty dollars. I always responded by sending a thank you note that read:

Dear _____,

Thanks so much for the wonderful graduation present. It will be a tremendous help with college expenses in the fall.

God Bless,

Brandon

Granted, this is a rather short and sweet thank you note to write, and I was certainly grateful for all the wonderful financial gifts I received. However, after writing the same basic note over and over and O-V-E-R again, it gets repetitive and rather annoying. At one point, I was praying I wouldn't receive anymore checks as gifts so I could stop writing the thank you notes.

Even when my great aunt sent me the gift of a check in the amount of one thousand dollars, my five seconds of shear happiness were quickly shattered with the realization that not only would I have to send her a thank you note, but because of her generosity, I'd have to send an even LONGER thank you note. I never thought it was possible that receiving a check for a thousand dollars could ruin your day, but I can tell you from experience, it's possible.

Even though sending cards to people has never come naturally to me, it does come naturally to my mother. She views sending cards to those that are in dire need of receiving cards as her God-given duty. She will often go to the store and stock up on a variety of cards for as many occasions as she thinks are necessary. This includes birthdays, engagements, marriages, medical procedures, recoveries, or if the medical procedures don't go so well, deaths, funerals, and second marriages.

When my mother sends a card, she makes sure that she's sending the right card for the right occasion. After my mother finds the "perfect" card, she will sit down and write the most heartfelt words she can think up. She'll begin by writing, "Your friendship means more to me than you'll ever know. I'm a better person for having met you." At this point, if my father and I happen to make the mistake of walking into the room and talking within ear shot of her, she'll look up and snap, "Will you two loudmouths shut up for two seconds! I'm trying to write!!" At this point she'll get back to her card and write, "You've taught me about the importance of showing compassion to my fellow man."

Don't get me wrong. If someone I know is sick or having problems, I'll stop what I'm doing and say a prayer for them on the spot, but it's not my nature to hitch a ride to the nearest Hallmark store and browse through the card aisle for over an hour, reading the inside of every card, and through all the beautifully written poetry and well-wishes, find the right card that lets that special person know I'm thinking of them. At best, I might look around the card aisle and find the first card that says "Thinking of you" on the front and buy it (assuming it was on sale and the church will reimburse me for the postage ... and also for the purchase of the card, too).

As time went by, I became more comfortable sending cards to my deacon families, but one thing I was never comfortable doing was to call my deacon families at home and risk disturbing them. Since I don't drive, I certainly wasn't in a position where I could really visit people, either. This may have worked out better, though, because early on, I was warned by the other deacons that some older church members, especially "The Church Ladies," didn't like surprise visits from deacons, especially if their house wasn't clean enough to meet the criteria of what they consider to be a clean house or if they happened to have their hair in curlers. Some deacons who choose to embark on such dangerous expeditions have never been seen or heard from again.

*   *   *

Early on, I learned that all deacons in my church were also required to fulfill certain obligations, including serving as "duty deacon" in an assigned month. Part of the duties included unlocking and locking doors before and after church services. This sounds simple enough, but the problem was that my church is rather large with many doors, and to either lock or unlock all the doors I needed to was always time-consuming. Plus, when I locked up at night, I often found myself alone in very dark and scary places.

I want it noted for the record that I am not afraid of being alone in the dark. I am, however, afraid of thinking

I'm alone only to discover the whole time I was actually surrounded by the forces of evil previously concealed by the darkness. It's for this reason that whenever friends invite me to midnight campouts in overgrown cemeteries in the middle of the woods located next to abandoned insane asylums, I always respectfully decline the offer.

I remember my first night of lock-up duty. Following the Wednesday night prayer meeting while everyone was downstairs in the sanctuary during choir practice, I was alone in the upstairs wing of an adjacent church building walking alone very slowly in a dark hallway and thinking to myself, "You know, the next time I do this, I should definitely remember to bring a flashlight."

As I walked down the dark hallways, I checked empty Sunday school classrooms to see that everything was in place and checked the faucets in the restrooms to make sure they were turned all the way off. Of course, I made sure to knock on the door of the ladies' restroom first and announce I was coming in. If I didn't and I walked in on an unsuspecting lady, it could mean a fate far worse than what the previously mentioned forces of evil could ever do to me.

As I continued my rounds, I tried to remain calm by thinking about funny TV shows or movies I had recently seen, but all I could usually recall was every ghost story I had ever seen on reruns of *Unsolved Mysteries*. I reminded myself that ghosts aren't real and that the shadows I saw on the walls couldn't possibly be the silhouettes of any ghostly apparitions. Of course, by ruling out ghosts, it freed me up to imagine that the shadows resembled the silhouettes of the group of escaped serial killers I saw earlier that evening on the local news who were alive and well.

As I made my way back downstairs, I was relieved to finally see the light that shone from the other side of the doorway that led into the brightly lit hallway next to the sanctuary where the choir had been rehearsing. I swore the next time I had to do lock-up duty I would make sure I had two things available to me I hadn't had this time: 1. a flashlight, and 2. someone to hold the flashlight who wasn't me so I could stay home. I often had to settle for just the flashlight, though.

*   *   *

It says in Proverbs 3:5-6 (NIV) to "Trust in the Lord with all your heart and lean not on your own understanding; in all your ways acknowledge him, and he will make your paths straight."

I've learned that when walking in physical darkness, it's important to have a flashlight to see what direction to take. But what's even more important, when walking in spiritual darkness, it's crucial to let God be your light so He can reveal what direction He wants you to take.

Whether you're a child with a hundred dreams taking you in a hundred different directions, a teenager trying to figure out which college to attend and which field to major in, or perhaps even an adult who still doesn't know what you want to be when you grow up, let God lead you down His chosen path for your life while you faithfully trust Him to do so. Also, take time to thank God for all the blessings in your life, including the hard times that help make you stronger and focus your attention back onto the God who loves you unconditionally.

For years, I traveled down some confusing paths as I struggled to find a permanent job. Through times of rejection, I was reminded God is still in control and if He wanted me to work, He would bless me with the right job in His time. When that time finally came, I thanked God for answering my prayer and I vowed to be the best employee I could possibly be and have the best attitude possible.

Perhaps had this job not been a job in a retail store during the busy Christmas season, I could have kept this vow for more than five minutes.

Chapter 4
Life in The Store

WHILE WRITING THIS BOOK, MY goal was to fill the pages with the amazingly jaw-dropping details of every exciting, glamorous, and death-defying job I've ever had in my adult life.

Then I remembered I've never been very good at fiction writing.

The truth is, after finishing grad school, it took me two years to find a permanent job. In that time, job interviews were few and far between.

During that time, I published my second Christian humor book and decided that since I wasn't working I would use the free time to promote the book. Over the next several months, I sent over nine thousand promotional e-mails to churches and individual church leaders including pastors, associate pastors, youth pastors, secretaries, receptionists, and custodians.

This led to approximately thirty sales worldwide and several rude responses from pastors who felt led to inform me that the excerpts from the book I included in the e-mail (that were as G-rated as they come) were not appropriate humor and they were suspicious of my motives.

I politely responded by thanking them for taking the time to get in touch and reminded them that humor is a wonderful thing, even the Bible encourages it. All pastors need to develop a sense of humor and learn to laugh when it's appropriate and also encourage the members of their congregations to laugh with them. Those that don't will have their congregations laughing AT them.

I had even less success in my job hunt.

I considered going into teaching, but all this led to were polite letters letting me know my resume would be kept on file for a year. The one interview I managed to get at the local community college led nowhere.

I also considered going back to school to take additional courses so I would be qualified to teach certain subjects but eventually decided against it. With the courses I had already taken in grad school, the two most likely courses I would have ended up qualified to teach were history or English. I have never had any desire to teach any history course. As far as teaching English, it's bad enough having to correct all my own grammatical errors. Why would I want to spend hours at a time correcting the errors of dozens of students on top of it?

Another reason why I never seriously considered teaching English was because there are simply too many rules on punctuation to memorize. There are about forty rules for comma usage alone. I'm also too afraid to use a semicolon because I've never quite figured out what purpose it serves, and I'm too embarrassed to ask. As best I can tell, a semicolon is basically a fancy comma that thinks too highly of itself.

My parents also encouraged me to take additional courses so that I would be qualified to teach sociology, which is the study of humans and human behavior. Through the years, however, the more I've learned about human behavior, the less I understand.

Like many long-term job seekers, I thought going to a local job fair would help me find a job. If someone has never been to a job fair before, they may not know what exactly to expect because the name is misleading. When I used to think of a job fair, I had visions of a large county fairground with a carnival-like atmosphere with cotton candy and clowns passing out balloons. I also thought there were games you could play where instead of winning cheap prizes like stuffed animals you could actually win positions at companies, such as "Dunk the HR Rep, Win a Job!"

In reality, a job fair is an event where approximately fifty companies set up informational booths in a cramped gymnasium with about five thousand job seekers competing for jobs within these fifty companies, forty-nine of which are not currently hiring. If by some chance there is a clown giving out balloons, the balloons will likely have the phone number of the local unemployment office printed on them.

At one point I signed on with a couple of local temp agencies. All this landed me was a four-day job doing data entry work for an area charity during the holidays. I sat at a computer for nearly eight hours a day processing applications for families who were applying for assistance during the Christmas season. This would have been a rewarding job had I not noticed most of the people applying for help, who did not make much money, were actually making considerably more money than I was currently making. This led me to the realization that if my parents were not letting me live in their home rent free, it's likely I would be sitting there processing my own application.

Finally, two years to the month after finishing grad school, I landed a seasonal retail job that later turned into a permanent part-time job at a warehouse club that I like to simply call "the store." I was hired on as a product demonstrator.

The best way to describe the job of a product demonstrator is to say I worked in a promotional capacity. Sometimes I demonstrated products to customers by showing them how well the product works, such as leaving my fingerprints on a mirror and then demonstrating a particular brand of glass cleaner by cleaning off the fingerprints. I always liked this particular demonstration because in theory, I was getting paid for behavior as an adult that always got me in trouble as a child. I'm certain when my mother learned part of my job duties included leaving my fingerprints on mirrors, this caused her considerable turmoil. Like most of the mothers of the world, she has made it her life mission to keep me from ever leaving my fingerprints on anything, let alone getting paid to do it. I think she was a little relieved, though, when she realized that at least I had to clean off the same fingerprints all day long.

Mainly my job entailed talking with customers and telling them about the product I was promoting by passing out free samples of the product, which ranged from trash bags and razors to cereal bars and candy.

Though it wasn't my goal in life to become a product demonstrator, or as we are known by others in our trade, a professional gummy bear giver outer, I found the job rewarding. Through the experiences I've had while working in the store, I quickly learned what life is like for all the brave souls who choose to work in a retail setting. Here are some of the highlights:

The Interview: I learned that interviewing for a job in a retail store, or anywhere else, is like being a candidate running for public office whose sole purpose is to do what it takes to get the vote. You get dressed up in your best suit, show up early to meet with the person or persons interviewing you, and while they ask you numerous questions, you do your best to maintain eye contact with them and provide them with specific-sounding answers that don't reveal your personal opinion on anything. You take all sides of the issue by making such creative statements as, "I'm a firm believer in the concept of individualistic teamwork." You also learn to think on your feet because, unlike a candidate running for office, the questions are not given to you ahead of time and you don't have access to a teleprompter.

Orientation & Training: After I was hired, I reported for group orientation at 7:00 a.m. the following Monday. The night before was the first time in months I had set my alarm clock to wake me up and certainly the first time in years I had to set it to wake me up at 5 a.m. It didn't matter, though. I was so excited to finally be working that I didn't sleep at all that night.

During orientation, I was taught the history of the store, was given my name badge and locker combination (which only took me about a year to learn how to open), and learned about my benefit package, which was quite generous for a retail job. At the conclusion, the general manager came in to sit down with us and let us know how much we were valued as employees. He then went over the store's labor policy in a speech I like to call "Love Means Never Having to Say, 'Let's Unionize!'"

We also learned about "the culture" of the store which included wishing the customers a "Merry Christmas" since we were nearing the holiday season. This suited me fine because I grew up believing NOT wishing someone a Merry Christmas was politically incorrect.

As part of my training, I also completed a variety of computer courses on the store's online network that covered a wide range of topics from proper food safety to dealing with injured customers. Sometimes all I had to do was read brief statements about what I agreed to do and click on the screen where it said, "I agree to comply." I learned early on to be careful with this type of computer work because if I didn't fully read what I was agreeing to comply with, I thought there was always a chance I might unknowingly agree to sell my firstborn son to work in the store for a forty-year, non-negotiable contract. I assured myself this scenario was unlikely to occur, but if it ever did happen, at least I would have someone to carpool to work with eventually.

Some computer drills were more complex. For example, in one drill I learned about the dangers of sexual harassment in the workplace. It featured scenarios about what is and is not appropriate behavior, including what types of jokes were deemed acceptable and unacceptable. As a Baptist, the best way I can describe the drill is as follows: Any joke that you would tell inside the Baptist church is probably appropriate for the workplace. Any joke you would tell outside of the Baptist church, while standing in the parking lot after the church service, would probably be deemed inappropriate.

In another drill I learned about properly cleaning up hazardous spills. I learned there are certain steps an employee must take in properly dealing with such spills. First, it's important to identify the spill, which I guess means looking down and saying, "Yep, that's a spill, alright." Next, the spill must be guarded by that employee until someone, most likely a member of the maintenance crew, can be located to clean the spill. In theory, I could clean the spill myself, but all my life I have wanted to be able to say, "Sorry, that's not my department." By cleaning the spill myself it would rob me of the chance of ever saying that. If I did end up cleaning a spill, though, I learned I had to take protective measures, such as wearing gloves and face masks, but only for the most hazardous spills like bleach or battery acid. As cautious as I am, though, I would have worn gloves and a face mask to clean up a spilt can of Sprite.

Dress Code: Though we had a casual dress code at the store, my department fell into a different category. Because the professional gummy bear giver outers often served food to the customers, we were required to wear white shirts with black pants and black aprons. Whenever several of us were walking together, it looked like a scene in *March of the Penguins*. In fact, because of our dress code, we were nicknamed "the penguins."

"The penguins" may have dressed in the same colors, but we were never mistaken for members of a dangerous gang, especially when we wore our see-through disposable serving gloves and hairnets. Whenever I wore the hairnet, commonly known as the "penguin bandanna," it always ended up crooked and too low on my face. I was compared to Ruth Buzzi on more than one occasion.

Since I'm not a fan of handshaking, I did love wearing the disposable gloves, though. When customers shook my hand, all I had to do was simply take off the glove, put a new one on, and go about my business. Life seemed just a little brighter.

Working Weekends: When working in a retail store, especially part-time, employees must be willing to work the hours they are given, including working on the weekend. This can be annoying, but in time, most employees get used to it.

Recently, I worked three days in a row: Saturday, Sunday, and Monday. I've discovered that if Monday is the end of my work week, after awhile Mondays begin to feel like Fridays, which is a nice change. Even better, Tuesdays, which many argue have no feel whatsoever, begin to feel like Saturdays, which is an even nicer bonus.

I never got used to working on Sunday, though. As states have repealed their blue laws, many businesses are now open on Sunday. I think this is quite sad, because I, like many others, believe that Sunday was meant to be a day of rest and a time to spend with friends and family. In my case, I enjoy spending this time with my friends and family in church on Sunday morning.

Even though I was blessed with a wonderful supervisor who made sure I had some Sundays off, I still had to work on many Sundays, which for me, just isn't the same as sitting in church on Sunday morning, listening to the beautiful old hymns sung by the choir and hearing the convicting yet uplifting words of the pastor's sermon.

I also learned that when you begin to miss Sunday after Sunday, the people in your church begin to ask questions.

During the Christmas rush when I worked for eight Sundays in a row, my parents were left at church with the unpleasant task of assuring other church members that I had not converted to atheism, or worse, had committed the unspeakable act of "shopping around" at other area churches.

I realize people in certain professions have to work on Sundays, but personally, I don't believe every business has to be open on Sunday. I believe a business that closes on Sunday, such as Chick-fil-A, can still do just as well financially, if not better, as the ones that remain open. Some customers actually prefer to shop at businesses that choose to close on Sundays.

As long as people shop and eat out on Sundays, there will always be a need for stores and restaurants to remain open. Even many regular churchgoers, including myself, shop and eat out on Sunday. Granted, we may not be working, but we still contribute to the need to keep those stores and restaurants open and their employees working on Sunday, which may keep them from being able to go to church themselves, or just spend more time with their own friends and family. I realize this isn't a popular statement to make, but if four years of high school taught my anything, I'm not a popular guy, and that suits me just fine.

Meetings: Unlike some workers, I always loved employee meetings. Since I worked in a job where I was on my feet over seven hours a day, I always looked forward to meetings. For a few precious minutes, not only did I get to sit down, but since I was on the clock, I was paid to sit down.

All the professional gummy bear giver outers knew this,

and we were usually not in any hurry for our meetings to finish early. In fact, we were not above trying to find creative ways to keep our supervisor talking so we could avoid going back out on the sales floor any sooner than necessary.

It's very reminiscent of my high school days. At the start of every school day Mr. Strickland led us in daily devotions, which was closely followed by a time to discuss current events. We often discussed the most pressing issues of our time, which for us was that year's UNC-Chapel Hill basketball season.

If the Heels weren't playing, we tried to find something else to talk about because everyone knew after the current events period concluded, Mr. Strickland would make us get to work.

Through the years, many students found creative ways to keep Mr. Strickland preoccupied in order to stretch the current event period out. One of the best ways was to ask him to tell a story. It became a little game among us students to see how long we could stall him before he made us get to work. Mr. Strickland knew this, but was willing to play along when he was in a good mood, which was most of the time.

My classmates and I enjoyed hearing Mr. Strickland's stories, which were mostly stories about former students from years gone by or from his days as a criminal investigator in the military back in the Seventies. He told us the same stories over and over again (we even numbered these stories in our heads), but they were usually interesting. Better yet, they were always time consuming.

He told us serious stories about life and death, such as being on the scene of a fatal drunk-driving accident, or funny stories about searching a home for drugs during Christmas time. The Christmas drug bust story, or as we liked to call it, Story #362-K7, was a personal favorite.

Mr. Strickland and his fellow officers had been searching a home for illegal drugs. Try as they might, they found nothing. Just as it looked like all hope was lost, one of the officers, perhaps Mr. Strickland himself, got the idea to search through the wrapped Christmas gifts under the Christmas tree. I may be wrong, but I believe they even allowed the young child who lived in the house with his parents to open the gifts, which when unwrapped, revealed a large quantity of drugs. I always wondered if, when the shocked and presumably disappointed child opened his drug-filled Christmas gifts, he turned to his parents and said, "Cocaine AGAIN?? You gave me this LAST year! I wanted a *Starsky and Hutch* lunchbox!"

Our supervisor never told us any drug-related stories, so we had to settle for hearing about the importance of properly calibrating the food thermometers. However, when my coworkers and I worked together, we could get her to talk about that for at least fifteen minutes. I know Mr. Strickland would be proud.

Evaluations: Evaluations fell into the same category as meetings because, like meetings, I was paid to sit during the evaluation. But unlike meetings, evaluations were more of a concern because the outcome of the evaluation would determine how many more meetings I'd be getting paid to sit through in the future.

At my last evaluation, I sat down with my supervisor and she handed me a copy of the evaluation form. This was a standard evaluation all employees must go through and each individual employee's performance can fall into one of five basic categories. The interpretations of these categories are my own interpretations and do not necessarily reflect the views of the store I work for or the store's parent company, Stores, Inc.

The first category was "Below Expectations." This could be interpreted: "Apparently you don't like the prospect of receiving a paycheck as much as you say you do."

The next category was "Development Needed." This could be interpreted: "If you want your paycheck to remain as large as it is, you'll do as we say."

This was followed by the third category, "Solid Performer." This could be interpreted: "You may not make a lot of money, but you're worth every penny of it."

The fourth category was "Exceeds Expectations." This could be interpreted: "Keep working as hard as you have been and there may be a forty cent an hour pay raise coming your way!"

The fifth and final category was "Role Model." I was told that it's very hard for employees to make it to this category. "Role Model" can likely be interpreted: "Unless your boss needs a heart transplant and you're willing to donate your own, good luck in ever achieving 'Role Model' status."

After my supervisor and I discussed the five categories, a member of management came in to go over the evaluation with us. He told me how he felt I was doing in my job (I was a "solid performer" in almost every category, I might add) and we discussed my potential future career at the store. These types of conversations would lead to question-and-answer sessions about my future employment goals. This is where my vision problems always seemed to creep into the conversation. The question might be raised, "Brandon, do you think you would ever feel safe driving a forklift?" My most likely response would be, "If you were to die today in a freak forklift accident, do you know where you would spend eternity?"

If the evaluation is going well, and if it's a slow day in the store, an employee might try to keep his or her boss talking for a long time to avoid having to get back to work right away. I once heard a story about a retail worker who had an evaluation, and during the evaluation, his manager became preoccupied and began talking to his supervisor. The employee wasn't even sure they knew he was still in the room, but since he was being paid to sit indefinitely, he wasn't about to interrupt their conversation. The manager began telling a story about the time years earlier when he had the opportunity to take an attractive woman out to dinner. He was not feeling well at the time and didn't feel like going out, but she persisted. Though he was reluctant to go, he agreed to take her out. Long story short, the evening concluded with him and his date riding a city bus and him getting sick and throwing up on the bus...and also on his date. Ironically, after the incident she still was interested in seeing him. So, to all the guys out there, don't let a little thing like puking on a girl ever stop you from asking her out again. If this story is indeed true, that manager is a man who truly deserves to achieve "Role Model" status.

A Day in the Life of a Professional Gummy Bear Giver Outer: I've already mentioned my basic job duties, and now I'll discuss the specifics:

On an average day, I left home for work about twenty-five minutes before my shift began. Since I don't drive, my father usually drove me. He's a cautious driver, and with the flow of morning traffic, I usually arrived at work about fifteen minutes before my shift started.

When my father wasn't able to drive me to work, my sister Patti drove me. Her style of driving is slightly different from my father's. When she drives, we can leave the house five minutes before my shift begins, and by the time we pull into the store parking lot, I still have minutes to spare.

Patti is a woman who has never been known for her careful driving. Since I don't drive, I figure it's not my place to give driving instructions. Because I'm visually impaired, however, I do feel more than qualified to explain the concept of a "blind spot," specifically the kind that someone like Patti finds themselves in when tailgating an eighteen-wheeler, or on some occasions, driving directly underneath the trailer of an eighteen-wheeler.

After arriving at work and before clocking in, I would make one last pit stop at the restroom since I knew it would be at least a couple of hours before my first break. While in the restroom, I always took a moment to look at myself in the mirror. I know men have teased women for years for being too concerned with how they look, but truthfully, men are concerned about how we look, too. In some cases, if we're not concerned, we should be. When looking in the mirror, I took care of the basics like making sure I didn't have any toothpaste on my lips or that my hair didn't look like it had gotten into a fight with static electricity and had lost. When some people look at themselves in a mirror, they want to look good. My goal is to look good enough to not frighten small children and animals.

It's frustrating when you can't always look as good as you want to. For years I've had issues with acne. I hate admitting this because I'm twenty-nine years old and I equate pimples with being a teenager. By the time someone turns eighteen, I think it should be biologically impossible to get pimples.

Why do we get pimples anyway? I have a theory that pimples are a punishment from God for the sins of Adam and Eve in the Garden of Eden. I think there may even be a verse in the Bible that says, "Woe unto your children for your sins. Beginning in their twelfth year they will be cursed with blemishes on their face which will serve as a remembereth of the 'blemishes' you have committed against me."

Why is it that those of us who get pimples always seem to get them at the most awkward moments and in the most awkward places? Why is it always Christmas time when I get a pimple on the tip of my nose and why is it there's always someone around singing *Rudolph the Red-Nosed Reindeer* at that time? Sometimes I wonder if that's even a real Christmas song or just a creative way to make fun of us "facially impaired" individuals who suffer from pimples.

After leaving the restroom, I walked to the break room and headed straight for the time clock. The second my shift began, I clocked in. When I first started working in the store, the employees were given more leeway about clocking in, and we could do so a few minutes before our shift began. It didn't take long before the management began cracking down on employees who were clocking in early and not immediately getting to work. Instead, people were getting paid while they sat in the break room reading the newspaper, grabbing a soda from the vending machine, and walking out to the parking lot to give their car a tune up and lube job.

I've never been a big fan of the time clock, but I've

gotten used to it. At first, when my shift began, I clocked in by swiping my name card, which scanned the bar code on it and it was accepted.

In time, though, the powers that be decided this way of clocking in might cause confusion for any employees who may not swipe their card properly or forget to swipe it at all. So, to make clocking in easier, now all I have to now do is swipe my name card and press the "clock in" button. If it doesn't accept me, all I have to do is a request override procedure. Then I locate the name of the manager that asked me to work. If I don't find his name on the first list of names, I punch the "more" button to go to the next list. When I do find the manager's name, I punch the button beside his name, punch in the time my shift ends, then indicate if that's A.M. or P.M., review the information, confirm the information, and that's it. My badge will be accepted and I can start work.

It's progress at its best.

After clocking in, I walked over to my supervisor's desk, also known as the central headquarters of the professional gummy bear giver outers. I searched through that day's paperwork to find my name and what product I would be promoting that day. My goal was to sell as many units as possible of the assigned product.

Sometimes I promoted products that were familiar to customers, such as Cheerios or Skittles. At other times, I got the chance to promote new products that people had yet to hear about, like Chocolate Sprinkled Prune Bites, the candy sensation "Made for Regular Folks to keep 'em *Regular* Folks."

I had a set goal for every product I sold. For the Cheerios, I might have had a goal of selling fifteen boxes.

For Skittles, it could be twenty boxes. For products like Chocolate Sprinkled Prune Bites, the likely goal would be five hundred boxes (before lunch).

One of the most enjoyable parts of my job was passing out free samples of products. It's fun to work in a store where I was allowed to open the merchandise. I was basically getting paid to do in this store what could get me arrested elsewhere.

Customers loved free samples, especially the dessert items. I will admit, though, I always had mixed emotions about customers pointing at me and exclaiming, "Hey, it's the 'cream puff' guy!" In their defense, though, they had no way of knowing that was my nickname back in high school (well, one of many).

Customers were allowed to come back for samples as often as they wanted to. The only major rule the store has about serving customers was that we weren't allowed to give out samples to children unless we received parental permission beforehand in case the child had any food allergies.

The professional gummy bear giver outers always took this rule very seriously, and most parents were more than happy to oblige. It always amazed me, though, how some parents got an attitude when they had to walk just a few feet over to where I stood to give their permission before I served food to their children. I thought since I was trying to keep their kids from ingesting something that could possibly kill them, they would have shown more gratitude. I was helping to keep their children alive so they could grow up to cop an attitude when I asked their permission to serve their children as well.

Despite how some parents acted, we always tried to be

polite and courteous to both the parents and the children. However, we did learn one lesson: If you see someone you presume needs parental permission before you can give them a free sample, when you respond by saying, "I need to have your mommy come over here first and say it's ok," make absolutely certain that it really is a child you're talking to and <u>not</u> an adult female who is just very short, as one of my coworkers found out the hard way. She might have been able to convince the lady she was only kidding, but since she was speaking to her in baby talk at the time, she realized it was pretty hopeless by that point.

Starting my shift: Before going on the sales floor, I always followed certain procedures. First, I stocked up on supplies for the day. This included plates, a bottle of sanitizer, napkins, serving cups, a serving bowl, and most importantly, a fly screen. If any flies buzzed around the food samples, I could use the screen to keep them off the food. This kept me from having to convince the customers that the tiny little black things they just ate in their trail mix sample were raisins.

While on the sales floor, I used a stainless steel cart that I wheeled on and off the floor when needed, which was always washed and sanitized thoroughly before and after my shift. If there were no carts available, I used a card table with a table cloth on top that stayed on the sales floor during the entire shift. The table cloths and plates I used on the table had to be "season specific." If it was the week of Halloween, for example, I could not use a table cloth with pictures of pilgrims on it or a plate with little cupids in diapers brandishing bows and arrows with hearts, unless I could somehow convince my supervisor that it was actually people dressed up like pilgrims and cupids who were going to a Halloween costume party.

As soon as I was set up on the sales floor, I then located my assigned item on the shelf. After locating the item, I would take several boxes or bags of it back to my designated location so that if customers liked the sample of the product I served them, they could pick up a box or bag of it at my location and not have to walk over to the shelf. When trying to sell impulse items, every second counts. By the time a customer is half way to the shelf, they may lose interest in the product and change their mind about buying it. This didn't happen as often with Cheerios or Skittles, but when promoting the Chocolate Sprinkled Prune Bites, if someone ate too many samples, that person may not have time to make it to the shelf.

Promoting Products: In regards to how I promoted certain products, I learned a little creativity can go a long way in attracting the customers' attention.

Once on a slow Sunday morning I was giving out samples of string cheese. Since I couldn't be at church that Sunday, I decided to pass the time by making my own church using the string cheese and the toothpicks I was using to stick into the cheese in much the same way children play with tinker toys. What began as a one-room church house eventually grew into a massive three-story worship center with a sanctuary large enough to seat thousands, multiple Sunday school rooms, media center, and a gymnasium, also known as a "family life center," if you want to use the spiritually correct term

Needless to say, the customers were impressed. I could tell by the way they kept pointing at my sculpture and whispering to each other, although that still doesn't explain all the snickering.

Before I had time to build the Olympic-sized Baptismal pool, the string cheese church began melting from the heat and was breaking apart. I had to think quickly and turn the structure into something else. As the day went on, my church turned into a lunar space vehicle. When that fell apart, it became a model of an atom. When I couldn't get the atom to stand upright any longer, I stuck two more toothpicks into it, called them antennas, and told customers it was some type of unidentifiable venomous insect.

When I told my mother later that evening about First Church of String Cheese, I could tell she was a little annoyed. It wasn't because she felt what I had done was sacrilegious, but rather she couldn't believe I spent the whole day at work getting paid to play with my food. This was yet another behavior she has devoted her life as a mother to stamp out.

Of course, I used other approaches as well to promote products. For the Chocolate Sprinkled Prune Bites, I found that the best thing to do was take a couple of empty boxes of the Prune Bites, walk over to the restrooms, and place an empty box outside both the men's and women's rooms. When the customers walked by and saw the boxes, they would believe the product lived up to its slogan.

Dealing with Coworkers: One aspect of my job that I never fully got used to was the fact that most of my fellow professional gummy bear giver outers were female. I was one of only two men in my department. Though at times this proved awkward, such as when I had to do paperwork at my supervisor's desk and the only writing utensil I could find was a pen made to look like a fairy godmother's magic wand, I'll admit there were some definite advantages.

For instance, on those rare occasions when I needed to look in a mirror, I knew there was always one in the vicinity. If I couldn't find one hanging on the wall, all I had to do was call out, "Does anyone have a mirror?" Like clockwork, a half a dozen coworkers could reach into their purses at once and pull one out.

Another advantage was that I was usually the first person my female coworkers turned to when they had a serious problem because they knew that only a man like me could help them meet their needs. Generally, their needs ranged from needing me to hand them bowls from a high shelf because they were too short to reach it or opening the lid of a jar that was too tight. These were the moments where I excelled at my job. Even in today's troubled economy when thousands of people are losing their jobs everyday, I took comfort in knowing that as long as I was one of the few people in my department who wasn't afraid to kill a scary spider that was terrifying my coworkers, I was likely to always have job security.

Working with me also gave my female coworkers many advantages, too, such as providing them with a firsthand opportunity to see how the male mind functions in the workplace. For example, when opening a box of supplies, most women I worked with thought the best way to do this was by using a box cutter, or perhaps scissors. Men, however, instinctively know that box cutters or scissors aren't necessary when we can just as easily use our bare hands to open that box. Of course, by the time we finish opening it, it's usually no longer useful as a box, unless there happens to be some duct tape in the vicinity. If so, it's only a matter of seconds until most men can remedy the problem by using the duct tape to repair the box, and in such a way that it now looks like a piece of modern art worth millions of dollars.

Of course, I also learned about how the female mind works, too. For example, I learned there is a big difference in how my female coworkers view the act of getting a haircut. For a man, a haircut is usually just that, a haircut, nothing less or more. When I get my hair cut, all I ask is two simple things: First, don't keep me waiting to get my haircut any longer than necessary because, like many men these days, I go to a hairstylist, and there are usually only so many magazines in the sitting area that appeal to male customers. I don't want to get stuck waiting for half an hour having nothing to read but magazines with article titles like *Don't Wait Too Late To Debate Whether Your Date May Become Your Mate and You Procreate and Seal Your Fate.*

Second, when the stylist cuts my hair, I want to be able to sit there and whine about all the problems in my life that I whine about every time she cuts my hair. Instead of spending a hundred dollars an hour to talk to a professional therapist, it's far more cost-effective for me to spend twelve bucks and get a haircut out of the deal. It's just as important that my stylist listen to me complain about my life while resisting the urge to use the scissors in her hand for evil instead of good.

Getting back to the subject at hand, though, for a woman, getting a haircut usually means much more. It can be viewed as a life-changing decision that could alter her destiny. Many women view going to a hairstylist in the same way a patient visits a medical specialist to have an operation. If the "operation" (the haircut) is a success, the woman will come to work very happy. The mood will be light and there will be joy throughout the land. If, however, the "operation" is a failure, and the haircut doesn't turn out well, the woman's response will be much different. In this case, there will be fear throughout the land. The mood will be heavy, and it will be declared a day of mourning where any flags in the vicinity will be flown at half mast. This usually results in the woman running into the ladies' room in tears, with ten other female coworkers following behind. They will each do their part to console their upset coworker as they struggle for air in a bathroom slightly larger than a phone booth.

I suppose I could conclude this section by discussing what it's like working with women who are constantly on diets, but I would rather spend my time doing something less potentially life threatening, like trimming my nose hairs with my box cutter. (Hey, it's not like I actually use it to open boxes, right?)

*　　　*　　　*

Because I worked in a profession performed mainly by women, sometimes I felt as if I needed to change my sales approach to make it sound more masculine.

Once I was promoting a brand of paper plates that had the slogan "Incredibly strong, Uniquely elegant." As a guy, I felt a little uncomfortable hearing the words "uniquely elegant" come out of my mouth. I decided to change the slogan to something more masculine, hence the new slogan, "Incredibly Strong, RUGGEDLY elegant."

Perhaps the most difficulty I ever had was promoting products that appealed to more women than to men. For example, once I was assigned to promote a brand of body wash. I knew I was in for a challenge when, at the beginning of my shift, I had to ask my supervisor, "What exactly is body wash?" She explained it to me, and as best I could tell, body wash is basically soap in a bottle you lather up with in the shower. This must be what we guys call "a woman thing" because the only body wash I use in the shower is a bar of soap.

I tried my best to attract the customers' attention by asking them if they would like to smell the body wash. I tried getting in touch with my feminine side (which isn't too difficult when you wear an apron for a living) and called out to lady customers, "Excuse me, ma'am, would you like to experience a bold new fragrance of body wash that has a whimsical aroma of cucumber and croutons?" What I wanted to say was, "Hey, lady! Come over here and get a whiff of this! Have you ever gotten into the shower and thought, 'Gee, I wish I could smell more like a garden salad.' Well, NOW you can!"

Why do women use these types of products anyway? I want to say to all the women out there who use fragrances designed to make them smell like food products, at least find a product that makes you smell like prime rib or a baked potato. If you're married, your husband will appreciate this. They say a way to a man's heart is through his stomach, so if you smell like something he would order from the menu at a steakhouse, it may help rekindle the romance in your relationship.

Another product I promoted that I deemed rather feminine was something called body mist, which is also made to help you smell better. It does smell good, and I'm certain it's a terrific product, but in my opinion, this is yet another product whose name sounds like a medical ailment

(e.g., "Poor Aunt Gladys. As if the chronic Wikipedia wasn't bad enough, now she's been giving off body mist which requires her to see a dermatologist.")

When promoting such items, to avoid being accused of discrimination, I spoke to many male customers, too, albeit reluctantly. Here's another tip for any man working in a retail job normally held by women: Never attempt to sell a group of men who happen to be U.S. Marines ANY deodorant that makes them smell like rose petals after a rain storm. It's not pretty.

*   *   *

When trying to sell certain products, regardless of whether or not they were gender specific, I was more than willing to use the "scare tactic" approach. My goal was to convince customers their decision whether or not to buy certain products could mean the difference between life and death (a sales pitch similar to a hellfire and damnation sermon).

I found it the easiest to use scare tactics when promoting products designed to keep you healthy. Since I hate germs, I went all out on these types of sales pitches.

Let's say I was promoting facial tissue. First, I offered to let the customers have a free tissue. Then, as they blew their nose, I stepped far enough away so that any substance that came out of their nose couldn't reach my body. My goal was to stand close enough to the customer that they knew the sales pitch wasn't over but still remain far enough away that I wouldn't catch any infectious disease they may have, thus fulfilling the guidelines recommended by the Centers for Disease Control.

Next, I told the customer the box of tissues (or since I

work for a warehouse club, I should say the ten boxes of tissues that couldn't be sold separately) could be placed in the various rooms of their homes. If they or their children got sick, they could all stay in their own rooms and wouldn't have to walk all over the house spreading their germs as they tried to find a box of tissues. This would help to keep the rest of their family healthy during the next outbreak of swine flu, chicken flu, gnu flu, small lapdog flu or whatever strain we're hit with at the time.

I used a similar approach when promoting cleaning products. When promoting cleaning wipes, I told customers that it's important to have such products to disinfect surfaces of harmful germs that could put them or their loved ones in the hospital. For this sales pitch to be successful, I learned it was important to use the words "loved ones," "hospital stay" and "all your fault" as much as possible. I especially loved promoting cleaning wipes to the many military personnel who shopped in our store. These brave men have been trained in a variety of combat techniques and would approach the enemy without blinking an eye, but probably wouldn't think twice about cleaning surfaces. After I shared the dangers of salmonella, however, I had many of them more afraid of a approaching a cutting board with raw chicken juice on it in their own kitchen than they would be about approaching a cave in the hills a foreign country that is filled with armed members of a known terrorist group.

Sometimes I discovered my sales pitch went a little too well. When I told certain customers that the cleaning product I was promoting could easily remove a variety of stains, especially unwanted blood stains, some customers seemed a little *too* excited. Sometimes I wondered if I had unknowingly become an accomplice by selling the customers a product that helped cover up a crime scene. It wouldn't have bothered me so much had it not been for the fact that these were some of the same customers I had sold a box of extra strength and super absorbent trash bags the week before by showing them how strong they were by standing in them.

Dealing with Customers: It's impossible to write about what working in a retail store is like until I get more in depth about the types of customers I encountered on a daily basis.

Most of the customers that I served daily were polite individuals. They referred to me as "Sir" (or "Ma'am," if my hairnet was on and they weren't sure). They had also been taught the importance of saying "please" and "thank you" at some point in their lives and had not forgotten that lesson.

Not only were these customers polite, but they were fun to be around. Say if on a given day I happened to be passing out samples of dog treats, a couple could walk by me and I might say, "Excuse me, ma'am, would you like a treat for your dog?" The lady customer would then turn to her significant other, smile, and reply, "No thanks, he's already has his fill."

Ninety-nine percent of the customers I served helped to restore my faith in humanity. Then there was the group of customers I liked to call "the other one percent." They were the reason why I had lost faith in humanity to begin with. In actuality, the percentage of rude customers I dealt with was larger than one percent, but "the other one percent" sounds more dramatic than saying "the other five percent" or "the other thirteen-and-a-half percent."

Most customers I met were kind people who made me realize I was a better person the moment they walked into my life. "The other one percent," however, made me realize I was a better person the minute they walked away. I'm convinced God placed them in my life as a test to help make me a stronger person by not succumbing to the urge of jumping over my serving cart and strangling them.

Most customers were polite when they were sick and covered their mouths when they sneezed or coughed around me. "The other one percent," however, never covered their mouth when they sneezed or coughed. The closest they might come to being polite is if one of them threw up on my shirt and said, "Sorry, I was actually aiming for your shoes."

Most customers were willing to take the time to have an actual conversation with me, which often meant making the ultimate sacrifice of turning off their cell phone, maintaining eye contact, and talking to me. "The other one percent," however, couldn't do this because apparently they had been born with a hands-free cell phone attached to their ear and getting rid of it would mean having it surgically removed. Surgery was out of the question, though, since that might mean missing an "important" call.

Most customers showed enough courtesy that when they changed their mind about buying a certain product, they would put it back on the shelf where it belonged. "The other one percent," however, thought it was easier to leave the item wherever they were standing at the time and figured someone else would take care of it. If, for example, they changed their mind about buying a bag of frozen fish, instead of walking back to the freezer section where they picked it up, they found it more convenient to just wrap the fish in a display of towels on the shelf next to them and leave it there. It would then be discovered several days later by an unfortunate store employee who only found the fish because of the smell it was giving off due to the fact we were in the middle of a heat wave and the store's air conditioner was broken.

Most customers were grateful to receive the free food samples I gave out, regardless of what food it was. "The other one percent, " however, became upset when we were not serving their favorite foods (as if we had any way of knowing they were on a strict beef jerky and ice cream diet).

The main reason many customers came into the store was to shop, and getting a free sample of food was just an extra bonus. "The other one percent," however, were the customers whose sole purpose for coming into the store was to eat whatever free sample was offered to them. Their philosophy was simple: "If it's edible and free, eat it. If it's not edible, but still free, eat it anyway." They could be shopping at the other end of the store, and in the midst of crying babies, announcements over the store's public address system, and even forklifts traveling back and forth to move merchandise, they could actually hear me opening a box of peanut butter crackers. Before I could even pour the crackers into the serving bowl, they were already standing at my cart. Some days when I returned from my break, I wheeled my cart onto the sales floor and they were already waiting for me.

When I told them I would be ready to hand out samples in a few minutes, they often just stood there and stared at me until I was able to serve them. Many times they wouldn't take their eyes off me, which always made me a little uneasy. It's similar to how that dog, Eddie, stared at Kelsey Grammar on *Frasier*. I'm convinced their sole purpose for getting out of bed that morning was to get a free mini éclair or a fiber bar, and they were not going home empty-handed. It was as if they had set out to fulfill a Biblical prophecy.

When I was finally ready to serve them, they would take the sample (or samples) of their choice and proceed to inhale it in front of me. On some occasions I think they ate the napkin that came with the sample. To watch them eat, you would think they had just been rescued from a deserted island and this was the first piece of food they had eaten in months. If the food sample was in a serving cup, sometimes they took the cup, stuck it on their mouth, and sucked down the sample as if they were sucking down Jell-O shots during spring break in Daytona Beach. Sometimes, for safety reasons, I stepped back a few feet. The professional gummy bear giver outers followed a simple philosophy: "Greet, tell, and sell." With some customers, though, it was more like, "Greet, Retreat, and Admit Defeat."

After they finished eating, if they still had the serving cup in their mouth, they often spit the serving cup into the trashcan next to my cart. If the serving cup didn't make it into the trash can, they usually left it on the floor and walked away, leaving me to pick up their mess. I would then take a napkin and pick up the serving cup, making sure not to touch the cup with my bare hands, similar to how bomb squads handle possible explosive packages.

*   *   *

The customers in "the other one percent" group were also the ones who took practically everything I said or did out of context, so I learned early on to be careful what I said to them. Otherwise, I should be prepared for some dirty looks and nasty comments from them, and this includes the lady customers. Allow me to give the following examples:

Me: "Ma'am, would you care for a sample of a breath mint?"
Lady customer: "Why? Are you saying **my breath** smells bad?"

Me: "Ma'am, would you like to smell this new body wash?"
Lady customer: "Why? Are you saying **I** smell bad?"

And of course, last, but certainly not least:

Me: "Ma'am, would you like to try a sample of this breakfast cereal? It's terrific for customers who are health conscious."
Lady Customer: "Why? Are you saying **I'm fat?**"

Here's a tip for any man who finds himself in these situations. If any woman ever asks you if her breath smells bad, or if she smells bad, and of course the kiss of death, if you think she is fat, NEVER say, "Well...," and then hesitate before you utter your next word. Doing so may cost you your life.

I should also mention that when promoting scour pads, NEVER tell certain women they're great for removing excess makeup.

I can sum up my experiences with "the women of the other one percent" with this story. Once while passing out free samples of a product and giving my enthusiastic sales pitch, a woman walked up to me and said, "I just want a sample. I don't want to hear what you have to say." It had been a long day, and I replied, "Well, that's great, because frankly I'm tired of saying it." Some days I grew to hate the sound of my voice even more than the customers did. By telling me not to speak, little did she know she actually did me a favor.

To be fair to the women, there were quite a few men in "the other one percent," too.

One day I was promoting a stapler. I showed how it worked by stapling pieces of paper that were lying flat on my sales table. Then, to demonstrate the staple remover, I removed all the staples I accidentally stapled into the tablecloth without ripping the cloth anymore than I already had. The next morning while promoting a brand of breakfast bar, a gentleman who had been in the store the day before walked up to me and asked, "Where are your staplers?" I said, "Sir, that was yesterday. Today I'm doing the breakfast bars. Would you like a free sample?" He then proceeded to eat his sample of breakfast bar. When I asked him how he liked it, he responded, "I think I would rather have eaten the stapler."

The worst experience I had with a male customer was during a store-sponsored tasting event, known as "The Taste of the Store." For these events, the professional gummy bear giver outers served more free food samples than usual on a variety of items. We were viewed by the customers as waiters and waitresses whose sole purpose was to serve them as much free food as they wanted as quickly as possible. This wouldn't have been so bad had store policy not prohibited us from accepting tips.

Customers came out of the woodwork for the tasting events. Many brought their immediate families and their extended families. Sometimes they even brought the pets of their extended families. They could come back as often as they wanted for free samples, but I believe some customers wore disguises so they wouldn't be recognized, and we wouldn't be as reluctant to serve them their twelfth helping. Why they didn't realize that when wearing a fake beard or mustache they shouldn't wear a mini skirt and high heels at the same time is beyond me.

The tasting events were always stressful, and during such days, I often questioned why I ever went into this line of work. Now, this is where a particular male customer enters the story. It was during an extremely hectic point of the tasting event where I was exhaustively serving free samples of chicken salad on crackers to the customers. At this time, an older gentleman who apparently knew me and my background (though I can't say for sure who he was since I meet a lot of people in my job) approached me while waiting for his free sample. This man actually had the nerve to say to me that I must really enjoy working at the store because with my level of education, this isn't what he thought I'd do with my life.

Translation: "You went to graduate school for this?"

I told him that I loved my job and it had wonderful benefits.

Translation: "I hope chicken salad is the new miracle cure for wrinkles, because if you're not out of my sight within two seconds, you're going to be wearing it as a face mask."

If my boss happens to be reading this, for the record, I never gave into the temptation of throwing food at any customer. I was taught it's not a sin to be tempted, but only when you yield to the temptation. With God's help, I never yielded … but man, was I tempted.

*   *   *

Let's talk about "the children of the other one percent." Although most customers who brought their children to the store had taught them the importance of staying close to their parents and not running off, the "other one percent" had no problems whatsoever letting their children run wild through the store. In some cases, I think some parents even brought a stopwatch to see if their children could beat their previous best time for running wild through the store.

"The other one percent" rarely, if ever, punished their children. If they tried to, here's how the scene usually played out. First, the parent would inform the child in the scariest voice possible that if they didn't start behaving immediately that they would be sorry. This usually occurred approximately three feet away from where I was standing, which left me within earshot of the whole ordeal. If the child continued acting up, such as continuing to jump on a display of mattresses, ripping the heads off stuffed animals in the toy aisle, or swiping ketchup packets from the store's café, smearing it on their faces, and running around shouting, "I'm bleeding!," the parent would say, "That's IT!!! You're in trouble, now!!" Most children didn't respond too kindly to this threat. At this point, the child would let out a high-pitched scream which served as a war cry signaling all the other unruly children in the store to follow suit. Many parents, however, were completely oblivious to this high-pitched screaming. I always wondered if the child was screaming at a frequency that could only be heard by dogs and overworked store employees. Sometimes I've wanted to ask their parents if they have any knowledge of the Scriptures, because their child may be "the beast" referred to in the Bible.

Slow Time and Breaks: There were days at work where I never got a minute to myself. Other days I got too many minutes to myself. During slow days when there weren't many customers, I tried to find ways to fight the boredom. I came up with lots of great ideas, but most of them involved having paramedics on stand-by. This may be why my idea for all the store employees going back to our warehouse for some friendly forklift drag racing was shot down by the management.

Because my job required me to stand in the same aisle most of the day, I was rather limited in what I could do to pass the time away. Sometimes when there was no one around, I would see how long I could stand on one foot and keep my balance without falling over. My record for standing on my left foot is twenty seconds and for standing on my right foot is just under fifteen seconds. My record for standing on both feet without falling over is three hours and seventeen minutes.

Even when I was bored, I learned to look busy since some bosses view yawning on the job as a criminal act. Sometimes I walked down my assigned aisle and used my finger to point to random price signs and remained standing there, not taking my eyes off the price signs. That way, if my boss spotted me, it gave the impression I was comparing prices and familiarizing myself with the inventory. Sometimes I walked down the aisle and removed empty display boxes once filled with merchandise to make the displays look more presentable. If I were spotted at a display where there were no empty boxes to remove, I stood there and began to make random arm movements designed to give the impression that I was getting ready to arrange the merchandise on the shelf to make it look better. These types of hand gestures are the same ones used by some of our nation's most talented and annoying street mimes.

When I wasn't on the sales floor, I was either taking a break or eating lunch. On an average day, I took two fifteen minute breaks and a thirty minute lunch. I stayed on the clock for my breaks, but store policy required me to clock out for lunch. The one time I forgot to clock out for lunch I was reprimanded by one of the managers. We went over the company policy about clocking out for lunch, and I had to sign a document stating that he had spoken to me and that I understood what I did wrong. He also informed me that if this happened again within a certain time period, I would have to sit down with my superiors for a discussion on the importance of clocking out for lunch. In short, my punishment was a firm verbal warning that if it happened again, I would receive yet another firm verbal warning.

A verbal warning is a far better punishment than I might have gotten from Mr. Strickland back in high school for a serious offense. Thankfully, most companies, including the one I'm privileged to work for, realize if a manager paddles an employee it could lead to a sexual harassment lawsuit.

When I clocked out for lunch, I often ate by myself in the store's café where I purchased my favorite in-store beverage, a Cherry Icee. Then I would pour a pack of Lance Crackers into the drink and eat the crackers with a spoon. This is an acquired taste that few people have caught onto. I believe if people would give it a try, though, Lance Crackers in a Cherry Icee could become as popular as salted peanuts poured into a Pepsi.

As I got to know my co-workers better, I became more sociable, and sometimes I would eat with them in the break room, that special place store employees view as an oasis away from the sales floor. It's hard to describe everything that goes on in the break room. It's truly a multi-purpose facility.

I believe the break room was designed as a place for co-workers to come together and complain about bad workdays, such as during "The Taste of the Store." Complaining about it with one another became known as "The Aftertaste."

Regardless of what we were complaining about or when we were complaining about it, after listening to someone else's complaints about their bad day, we often tried to outdo their story by going into explicit detail about how bad our day had been. At this point the old timers would speak up and tell everyone about how things had changed for the worse since their first days in the store. When I'm referring to the "old timers," I'm not referring to the ages of the employees, but rather how long they have worked there. An eighty-year old door greeter who has worked in the store for six months is still considered the "new guy," whereas a twenty-five-year-old customer service rep that has been there for five years is given the same level of respect as a military veteran who served in multiple wars.

During our time together in the break room, we often discussed the pressing issues of our time and put our heads together to come up with feasible solutions to fix all the problems in our world today.

Once, we got into a lively debate about the state of our nation's prison system. We all agreed that it's just not right that prisoners have access to gymnasiums, unlimited reading material, and cable television. The cable television issue really irked us because, at the time, we didn't even have cable television in the break room. At the moment I'm writing this, we still don't have cable television in the break room, or a television at all, for that matter.

We all agreed we're tired of watching the local news and seeing mug shots of criminals who just stand there with big dumb grins on their faces because they think jail will be like a trip to a Caribbean resort at the taxpayers' expense. We all agreed we need to make prison life seem less pleasant for the prisoners first and foremost by taking away the access to the gymnasiums, unlimited reading material, and cable television. We also agreed the media should wait to show their mug shots until after they have spent a considerable amount of time in jail without the gymnasiums, unlimited reading material, and cable television. Then we'll see if they're still smiling.

If we had more time to discuss this issue, I would have added that I don't think prisoners should be allowed to eat any junk food that is paid for by the taxpayers. I say if a prisoner can't live without his daily supply of sticky buns and cheese doodles, well then, they should grow them themselves. Make 'em plant a sticky bun and cheese doodle garden and hope for the best. I also think that most violent prisoners shouldn't be eligible for parole until it comes time to harvest the sticky bun and cheese doodle crop, if you get my drift.

After such discussions, I've learned that when a group of hard-working store employees come together in a break room, in just ten minutes we can get more issues resolved than Congress. Unlike Congress, though, we have no vote on any decision regarding pay raises.

Finishing my shift: I always looked forward to the end of my shift in the evening. I enjoyed coming to work in the morning, but after being on my feet for over seven hours, I enjoyed leaving work just as much, if not more.

At the end of my workday, I gathered my supplies and wheeled my cart to the back of the store. I took my plates into our kitchen to wash and rinse them before placing them back on the shelf. Then, I washed my cart and placed it in its designated area. If no one was around, I hid all of the card tables in places where no one would think to look for them so that I may never again have to worry about convincing my supervisor that using a Frosty the Snowman tablecloth is appropriate on Independence Day during the store's "Christmas in July" sales campaign.

By now, I only had a few minutes left on my shift. I was always determined to stay on the clock for my entire shift so I could get paid for a full day's work. Many of my coworkers felt the same way, and we were willing to work together to earn every cent to which we were entitled. Here is the best way I know how to describe our style of teamwork:

Q: How many professional gummy bear giver outers does it take to change a light bulb?
A: Twelve

One to let everyone else know that a light bulb has burnt out.

One to give a second opinion by flipping the switch to make sure the first one was right.

One to say that the light bulb should be replaced.

One to recommend that before we replace the light bulb everyone should vote to see if there is enough interest in replacing the light bulb. (Apparently some of the professional gummy bear giver outers were also Baptists who realized nothing could be done unless it was voted on first.)

One to count the votes to make sure there are enough votes needed to pursue changing the light bulb.

One to volunteer to go find a new light bulb.

One to suggest that another vote be taken to see if that person is the most qualified person to find a new light bulb.

One to count the votes to see if that person was chosen to find a new light bulb.

One to stand guard in the dark room until the new light bulb can be found so no one will fall down in the dark and get hurt and the store can reach its goal of one-hundred eighty days accident free and we become eligible for the free steak lunch that we were promised six months ago.

One to screw in the new light bulb.

One to double check to make sure the replacement bulb is environmentally friendly so that we can give the impression we're doing our part to conquer the threat of global warming.

And, finally:

One to stand next to the time clock the entire time to make sure that the rest of the professional gummy bear giver outers don't finish replacing the light bulb one second before our shift ends.

*   *   *

The most enjoyable part of my shift was sitting down

at my supervisor's desk in the evening and working on that day's paperwork. This included writing down how many packages of my assigned product I opened to serve to the customers so we could keep track of our inventory. I was also required to write the comments that customers made that day about that product.

The amount of time I took to write customer comments depended on how much time I had left in my shift. To put this in perspective, let's say on a given day I was promoting a brand of Nut Clusters. If I only had a minute or so before I was supposed to clock out for the night, I might write something quick like:

"Customers loved the Nut Clusters! Most liked the taste and the price! Good seller!"

If I had ten minutes before my shift ended, for the sake of staying long enough to earn my entire day's pay, I might write something like:

"Most customers loved the Nut Clusters. Over the course of the day, I served over four hundred samples to just over one hundred people. Of that total number, approximately ninety percent of the customers loved the Nut Clusters, whereas ten percent seemed not to like anything at all about the Nut Clusters.

I was able to determine that the customers who chose not to purchase the Nut Clusters appeared to be very unhappy people, so I decided they were in need of in-store psychological counseling. Since I took one semester of general psychology in college, I felt I was qualified to lead the session. During one such session, I met a customer that we'll call "Bob," which works out great because his name really was Bob. As I tried to sell Bob a bag of Nut Clusters, he opened up to me about how he had just broken up with his girlfriend and that Nut Clusters was her favorite snack and he couldn't bear to even look at the bag. He also said that she smelled like rose petals after a rain storm so I decided this wasn't the time to try to sell him any deodorant, either.

It was at that time Bob broke down and began to weep openly. I tried to tell Bob that it was perfectly natural for a man to cry in public and it wasn't my place to judge him.

Anyway, Loony Bob cried for about five more minutes, and since he was scaring away my other customers, I convinced him this would be a great time to buy the ten pack of facial tissue which I figured would last him through the night, which he gladly did.

I began to feel good about myself, but then I realized that since I wasn't assigned the facial tissue that day, I wouldn't get any credit for that sale. Then I began to feel depressed myself and had to buy a pack of facial tissue for my own use, which now added up to two sales for which I wouldn't get credit, which caused me to sink deeper into depression.

I began to question my entire life up to that point and what my purpose is for living. I realized if my supervisor hadn't assigned me to sell these Nut Clusters, I would be so much happier now, but I can't change the past, only look ahead to the future which, for me, seems increasingly dark and barren. From here on out, I will have extreme difficulty even getting out of bed in the morning."

My comments were usually followed by a polite note to my supervisor asking for the next weekend off.

*   *   *

I spent many quiet evenings sitting at my supervisor's

desk finishing paperwork and getting ready to clock out for the evening. It was only a matter of time until I would be home in time for a late dinner of leftovers, purging my inbox of advertisements of ads for "little blue pills" with questionable reputations, and watching television with my parents and having our nightly debate in the middle of the crime drama we're watching as to whether or not the suspect the cops are interrogating looks just like my mother's urologist.

As I sat there, I often reflected on my experiences of the day. I'm ashamed to admit that I didn't learn the names of many of the customers I met, even though for the few moments we interacted with one another we were a part of each other's lives. Though the customers in "the other one percent" group gave me more grief than I needed, they were only a small portion of all the customers I served. Most customers, I discovered early on, were good and decent people.

There was the time I was on the sales floor when I was using a shopping cart to carry extra supplies. After I had emptied the cart, a woman approached me and asked if she could use my cart so she wouldn't have to walk all the way to the front of the store to get another one. I politely told her that I needed the cart later that evening to carry my supplies. Despite my refusal, she continued to ask me if she could have my cart. She was kind, but persistent. Finally, I agreed to let her have the grocery cart. She was so happy that she told me she would pray that God would bless me. I told her, somewhat jokingly, to pray that God would bless me with a girlfriend. To my surprise, right there in the aisle she began to pray out loud that God would bless me with a girlfriend in His time.

If that wonderful lady is reading this I should mention that to date, God has chosen to answer that prayer with a "Not yet." Please continue to keep me in your prayers. There may be an empty shopping cart in it for you.

Another time, while promoting dog treats, an older woman took the time to share a personal story about her experiences with me about her father and his hunting dogs. She told me that after he passed away, all of his dogs could sense he was gone for reasons unknown to them, but they all stayed together and acted as if they were waiting for him to return at any moment. Even after the dogs were given away to a nearby family, they ran away and returned to the spot where their former master always met them. This is just one of the many reasons why, as I grow older, my love for animals continues to grow because people have disappointed me on far more occasions than any animal ever has.

When promoting a battery-powered mop during the Christmas season, I met a mother of two small boys who took the time to listen to my sales pitch. She told me her two sons did all the mopping in their home. Moments later, her husband and two boys joined her. After explaining how the mop works by spraying the cleaning solution on the floor while you mop, her sons were amazed. At this point, one of the boys turned to his parents and exclaimed, "I want this for Christmas!" The mother agreed to buy the mop for her kids. I lifted one of the boxes containing the power mop from the sales display and placed it on the floor so her boys could carry their new mop home. By now the kids were so ecstatic their mother had bought them this mop for an early Christmas gift, they both came over and gave me a hug, which was quite a pleasant experience, if not a little surreal. Any mother who has raised her children to get excited when she buys them a new mop to use for a Christmas gift has definitely done something right.

Another time when I encountered an older couple, I asked the wife if she would like a free sample of the food item I was serving. She politely told me that because of her dietary restrictions, she couldn't eat the food. I turned to her husband and asked if he wanted to try a free sample. He said that because his wife couldn't have any that he wasn't going to have any either. It was such a simple yet profound lesson on making sacrifices for the ones you love, and I was glad he had been there to remind me of that.

One of my favorite experiences was observing two customers, who apparently had never met before until that day, talk with one another. When one of the customers, an older gentleman, learned that the husband of the younger woman he was speaking to was currently serving in the military, he asked her to please tell her husband how much he appreciated his service to our country. Then, he told her how much he appreciated the sacrifices that she as a military spouse had made herself, which allowed her husband to go off and serve our country. This man reminded me that we all need to take the time to thank our brave men and women in uniform for all they do to help keep us safe. He also reminded me that it's just as important to show support for their loved ones who are left behind for months at a time or longer and who, sadly, if their spouse makes the ultimate sacrifice for the country they serve, will forever be left behind.

These customers, all in their own unique way, reminded me of the principles of courtesy, loyalty, and love. These are the same principles that should be at the forefront of how we live our lives everyday.

On many occasions, customers took the time to share with me how God had blessed their lives. They often told me how God had been with them during difficult medical operations and how they were healed with the kind of healing that doesn't come from medicine. Many customers knew I was legally blind, and they told me how God restored their own eyesight in the past and how He was using them today.

They also reminded me that sometimes God has a special plan for others that doesn't always involve their being healed right away. It's important to remember that God is in control and that He knows what He is doing even if it doesn't always make sense to us. God's timetable and our timetable can be very different, but His is always the best.

I always enjoyed meeting these wonderful customers. Sometimes being with them for just a few minutes could turn a bad day around. They always seemed to appear on the days where I questioned why I was working in the store. I'm certain that God put them there to remind me that if I weren't working there, I would never have met them.

The professional gummy bear giver outers had been taught that a kind word and a friendly smile can go a long way in helping to keep customers coming back. More importantly, those same kind words and friendly smiles have the potential to make even the rudest customers see that God is working in our lives, and that includes "the other one percent." If they would give God a chance, He would work in their lives, too. Perhaps only then would they stop acting as if they could greatly benefit from eating an entire box of the Chocolate Sprinkled Prune Bites.

Chapter 5
Random Thoughts on Retail, Spirituality and Ham Biscuits

WHEN I WAS IN SCHOOL, I was blessed with an English teacher who was very passionate about her chosen profession, and she went to great lengths to teach her students the proper way of writing. To be more specific, one day in class after reading the rough draft of the book report I had been working on, she took it, held it up, and announced to the entire class, "This is an example of how NOT to write a book report!"

Needless to say, from then on out, she had lost my nomination for "Teacher of the Year." She did, however, know what she was talking about, and after I took her advice that day, my writing greatly improved, and I went on to pass her class.

Now that I'm a writer (or at least trying to give the impression that I'm one), I realize how important it is to follow the guidelines that were put in place by those first English teachers centuries ago who taught in cave schools and who were more than willing to embarrass their students by holding up their stone tablets and exclaiming, "Do you see little Og's tablet? This is an example of how NOT to write a report!" Teachers back then realized they could get away with a lot more with their students because they knew students like little Og wouldn't retaliate by letting the air out of their tires since the wheel had yet to be invented.

We've come a long way since English teachers graded their students' book reports with red chisels, but the basic rules for writing have remained the same. Good writers must adhere to the set of rules of proper writing if they want their readers to be able to make sense, enjoy, and even learn from their writings.

For anyone like myself who is writing an autobiography, it's just as important to follow the rules for good writing, such as refraining from the use of run-on sentences or making a habit of ending a sentence with a preposition (which according to some English instructors is considered a crime punishable by death in certain states). Unlike those book reports back in school, though, these days I have more freedom to express my own thoughts. I can do wonderful things in my own writings that I couldn't do in school, like quoting myself and never having to worry about adding a bibliography. I can give myself credit for my own quotes, which alleviates the fear of ever being accused of plagiarizing myself.

Of course, there are downsides to writing an autobiography as well. Most autobiographical writers quickly discover that some obstacles they face in their writing were never covered in their freshman English course.

Perhaps the most challenging part of writing an autobiography is deciding what tone the book should have. As I sit at my computer with my fingers pressed firmly on the keyboard ready to begin writing a new chapter, or sometimes getting ready to completely rewrite the previous chapter, I find myself asking the same question, "Should my writing be funny or serious?" When you develop a reputation for using humor in your writing, people expect you to write books that make them laugh. If you market your book as a humor book, it must be funny. In one sense, it's almost as if the more serious you are, the less seriously you're taken.

With so much tragedy and turmoil in this world, it's important for writers, especially Christian writers, to use the written word to bring their readers joy, comfort, and even a chuckle if possible. A good writer knows that humor can come out of serious situations, even the most tragic situations. A great writer, however, shows discernment when writing because sometimes it's simply not appropriate to joke about the tragedy around them.

Watch any television sitcom these days, and you'll see what I mean. If it weren't for the canned laugh track, you might not know you were watching something that is supposed to be funny. This may be why many sitcoms today are no longer taped in front of live studio audiences. The subject matter is so serious that most audiences would be too embarrassed to laugh at such topics as teenage pregnancy, sexually transmitted diseases, and addictions to prescription pain killers. If there were an audience, in order for them to know when to laugh, someone would need to hold up a sign that reads, "LAUGH!" after the actors said the "funny" lines. After hearing the joke, though, and seeing the "LAUGH!" sign, the audience would be thinking to themselves, "Are they serious?"

It's been said that when facing certain tragic situations,

or even just the petty and annoying ones, you can do one of two things: laugh, or cry. Whenever possible, I try to laugh about the situations I face. When I write about it, I try to use the same humor that helped get me through the situation because I want to show the importance of finding humor in the situations that we all face in our own lives.

Finding the humor in certain situations, however, isn't always possible. When I think about all the pain and sorrow in this world, I often find myself becoming upset to the point of becoming angry. Throughout my life in the church, the subject of anger has been the topic of more than a few Sunday sermons, and the question of whether or not it's wrong to be angry. I've reached the conclusion that anger in itself isn't necessarily a sin, but how someone chooses to deal with that anger can certainly fall into the "sin" category.

Over the years I've dealt with anger in both positive and negative ways. When someone has wronged me (or I thought they wronged me), I either asked God for the strength to go to that person to talk through our differences in a spirit of love and forgiveness, or I left God out of the equation and went to that person, and through my angry words and actions, I made a bad situation worse. This would later cause me to ask God for protection from that same individual.

It's for these reasons that I believe the written word can be better than the spoken word. When I say something hurtful to someone I can apologize for what I said, but I can never take it back. But when I write, I realize just how blessed I am to have access to the "Backspace" and "Delete" keys. On many occasions, what people read in my books is considerably more pleasant than what I originally typed in my rough draft. Sometimes it feels great to write certain things when I know I'm the only one who will ever read it. Even if I ever did write something that offended someone, I would rather have someone get upset and tear my book apart as opposed to having them tear my face apart, which is much harder to forgive.

*   *   *

When I was in school learning how to write book reports, I was taught to write the facts about my chosen subject and leave out my personal opinions, which was frustrating at times. It's for this reason that I enjoy writing my autobiography, because my personal opinions *are* the facts.

When I write about my life, I can write about the experiences that are most meaningful to me and what I learned from having to go through them. The experiences in our lives help shape who we are, and how we respond to our past experiences can help determine what experiences we may have in the future and how we'll respond to those experiences as well.

How people have responded to the stories I've written in my books has surprised me at times. Paragraphs or even whole chapters that I deemed "filler" material turned out to be the same paragraphs and chapters that many readers found to be the most enjoyable and even the most inspirational parts of my books. I have learned that I should never be afraid to write about what I have gone through in my life, because my words may be exactly what somebody needs to read at that time. A simple story in a book may lead to a profound lesson to the person reading it … and even to the person writing it. Allow me to clarify this through the following examples:

When I was a kid, I played quite a few children's games. One of my all-time favorites was a game that I like to call The Organized Gossip Game. The rules of this game are pretty simple: First, you get as many children as possible to form a circle. The larger the circle is, the more fun the game is, so it's a nice incentive to get as many children at once participating.

After all the players are in place, the children decide who will go first. The child who is picked starts the game by whispering a statement into the ear of the child he or she is sitting next to. Then that child whispers what he or she supposedly heard into the ear of the child he or she is sitting next to as well. This continues until the statement completes the circle. At that point, the last child is supposed to say out loud what was told to him or her and everyone hears whether it is the original statement or how close it is to being the original statement. Nobody knows for sure how the game will turn out, which is why it's so much fun to play.

Let's say you have a group of children who form a circle to play The Organized Gossip Game. All the children pick the child who will start the game. In this case, they choose little Sally. Sally starts the game by whispering into the ear of little Annie, "I hate dill pickles."

Next, Annie turns to little Joey and whispers into his ear, "I hate dill pickles." Joey, who hasn't quite grasped that the point of the game is to repeat word for word what is said, turns to little Heather and whispers into her ear, *"Annie* hates dill pickles."

Next, Heather, who never hears half of what anybody tells her anyway, turns to little Laura and whispers into her ear, "Annie hates *Bill Perkins*."

As luck would have it, their classmate, little Billy Perkins, is also playing the game as well.

Laura, who has the reputation of being the class gossip, forgets this is just a game and figures that if any girl in their class says she hates a boy, what she really means is she LOVES that boy. This leads her to eagerly turn and whisper into little Frankie's ear, "Annie *LOVES* Bill Perkins!"

The game continues, and each child in the circle hears what they have been told and decides to add their own spin to the information. By the time it's Billy's turn to play, he's been told "Annie LOVES Bill Perkins and they want to grow up to get married, have a house in the suburbs, and have ten children of their own!"

Billy, who happens to be sitting next to Sally on her other side, and who as you recall was the first one to play, knows for the sake of his reputation with the other guys, he must quickly eradicate any rumors of his potential upcoming nuptials with Annie. When it comes time for Billy to say out loud what was whispered into his hear, he thinks quickly, and says the first thought that comes into his mind:

"I hate dill pickles."

Both Sally and Billy are very pleased with the outcome of the game, but for very different reasons.

I've found that writing a book is similar to playing The Organized Gossip Game. When I'm sitting at my computer, my brain will either successfully send a signal to my fingers to begin typing the exact words I want to see on the computer screen, or there will be an interference that blocks that signal from correctly reaching my fingers. What I end up typing proves that something got seriously lost in the translation.

Of course, I'm referring to writer's block, a problem that can cause a writer as much grief as a cyclist suffering from paralysis or an opera singer suffering from laryngitis. Although for those of us who cringe every time we hear opera music, that last cloud may indeed have a silver lining.

When dealing with a case of writer's block, many times my prayer life quickly improves. By this point I'm more than willing to do a little plea bargaining with God. I'm certain many writers have begged God for the ability to come up with something to write about in exchange for agreeing to work in the foreign mission field in some desolate fourth-world country that hopes someday to be upgraded to third-world status.

Thankfully, I have yet to reach the point where I had to agree to work in a country where its citizens have overthrown the government and elected a toucan as their new President. Most of the time God helps me to realize that the best thing I can do to help get rid of a case of writer's block is to get away from the computer for a few minutes and take my mind off writing. It's only when I think about writing that I can't seem to come up with suitable ideas.

One thing that helps me to come up with ideas is allowing myself to daydream. For example, at the time I'm writing this chapter, which happens to be in early January, I find myself reflecting over the events of the past few weeks during the Christmas season.

The Christmas season means different things to different people. For some, it's the time of year when families and friends gather together in the warmth of their homes and gaze out the window and watch awestruck as snowflakes, in numbers too unfathomable to count, fall gently to the ground and create a blanket of pure whiteness that covers their once familiar surroundings. For those of us who live in Eastern North Carolina, we gather together to watch The Weather Channel and gaze at our television screens at the video footage of people gazing out their windows watching the fallen snow. Then we turn to gaze out our own windows and watch the rain fall to the ground and flood our once-familiar surroundings.

Others equate the Christmas season with Christmas decorations. In my neighborhood, the decorations are usually put up the day after Thanksgiving, and like clockwork, are taken down the day after Christmas. Thankfully, most of the homes are tastefully decorated. In many neighborhoods, though, it seems like there is always that one homeowner who has a knack for decorating their home for Christmas in such a fashion that the homeowner's neighbors know that the more decorations this person puts up, the more everyone else's property values will continue to go down.

To be fair, most of the time the Christmas decorations really aren't that bad if the homeowner takes them down just after Christmas or New Years. By the time Cinco de Mayo rolls around, though, Christmas decorations lose much of their original charm. That giant Santa Claus in the attic window overlooking the neighborhood may have brought a smile to the faces of the children who walked by on their way to school back in December, but after a few months, the children are now having their parents drive them to school because they are too afraid to walk pass the house because "Santa" keeps staring at them. The police may even be called in to investigate. If the homeowner is determined to keep Santa up at the window indefinitely, they should at least mount a shotgun in his hand to scare off potential burglars.

The Christmas season is also a time of parties and celebrations. Recently, I was invited to a church Christmas party at a popular area restaurant that has a reputation for serving some of the best country cooking that I have ever been privileged to eat. The menu includes such culinary masterpieces as fried chicken, mashed potatoes and gravy, macaroni and cheese, and my personal favorite, homemade ham biscuits. I would travel across the country to eat these ham biscuits, let alone across the county. Just thinking about eating a plateful of those biscuits makes my mouth water. After eating a plateful of those biscuits, I usually need to drink a lot of water, too, to help wash down every salty and delicious bite.

On the evening of the dinner, my parents and I left our home a half hour ahead of time to make it in time for our scheduled dinner reservations. The restaurant is located on the other end of the county in an area known as Back Swamp.

As you probably guessed, Back Swamp is pretty much a rural area, and before we left, we made sure to carry our cell phone with us. When traveling down country roads at night to get to such places like Back Swamp, it's always important to carry a cell phone. This is generally a good idea when your nighttime destination is named Back Swamp, Back Woods, Back Hollow, Back Forest, Back Hills, Back to Back Episodes, Back Lake, Back Marsh, or Back to Basics.

It's not my intention to make fun of people that live in

rural areas, though. Having lived within the city limits all my life, I've come to the belief that someone who lives in a place like Back Swamp is more likely to know his closest neighbor who lives half a mile from his home than someone who lives in a large subdivision within the city limits who probably doesn't even know the name of his next door neighbor who lives thirty feet from him. If you ever did get stranded in a place like Back Swamp, you would probably find that people there are often more willing to help you than in a city where the pace of life is more hectic and stranded motorists are viewed as an annoyance rather than a concern.

Thankfully, my parents and I arrived at the restaurant that evening without having to use the cell phone and made it just in time for dinner. We did, however, miss the hayride before dinner that was held on the property of the restaurant, which is also a popular Christmas tree farm. Neither my parents nor I ever intended to go on the hayride, though, because no one in my family has ever really enjoyed sitting in hay. Besides, it was raining pretty steadily the evening of the hayride, which meant we would have been sitting in wet hay. Sitting in wet hay isn't fun because the hay gets stuck to your body, and when you get off the hayride, you end up looking like a scarecrow.

As the evening went on, we had a wonderful dinner, and yes, the ham biscuits were just as good, if not better, than I described. The only complaint I had was with the tables in the restaurant. In many restaurants like this one that cater to large groups, to accommodate the most people in an enclosed space, many times the groups are seated at narrow, rectangular tables. This seating arrangement makes it difficult to carry on a conversation with anyone who happens to be sitting just a few chairs away. If two people want to talk to each other and they're not sitting next to one another, they have to bend way over the table to carry on a conversation. This is not only annoying to everyone at the table, but it also obstructs the successful passing of the ham biscuits.

After dinner, our group decided to head over to the onsite gift shop to do some Christmas shopping. This particular gift shop had a rather intimate feel to it. By "intimate" I don't mean romantic, I mean small. When in gift shops this size, shoppers must be careful. They can be so close to the merchandise that if they cough, sneeze, belch, or simply inhale too deeply, they may end up knocking down an entire display of glass nativity scenes with a combined retail value of a price just under the taxable value of their home. When that poor shopper writes a check for all the damaged merchandise, it serves as another reminder of what else the Christmas season means to many people: going into debt.

Shopping plays a big role during the Christmas season as many shoppers exhaustively search for that last-minute "perfect" gift. Those of us who work in retail consider the Christmas season the most stressful time of the year. By the time Halloween rolls around, we wish it were possible to flash forward to early January and skip the holidays altogether. During this time of year, there is no such thing as a slow day and customers tend to be far more stressed than usual, and even downright mean at times. I've heard that in some retail stores, when one employee tells another employee that a certain customer in the store has the Christmas spirit, "has the Christmas spirit" is the official store code for "Call the police, the suspect has a weapon."

Because of the holiday stress, someone working a retail job can find it very difficult to maintain a positive attitude. A positive attitude, however, can make a bad day at work much more bearable and even fun at times.

As a professional gummy bear giver outer, I was taught that whatever item I was promoting, I was to be as enthusiastic about it as possible. I promoted many products as the ultimate "stocking stuffer" that everyone would be thrilled to find in their stockings on Christmas morning, be it fruit candy or septic-tank cleaner. Septic-tank cleaner is really a great stocking stuffer. It's the gift that says to that special someone "Merry Christmas. It's time to clean up your act."

There are many other creative ways to promote products during the Christmas season. For example, when promoting headache medicine, a great way to sell it is to have the store play *Grandma Got Run Over by a Reindeer* repeatedly over the store's loud speaker. I have never actually been able to do this, but had I been, I'm certain I would have sold out of the headache medicine in record time. If *Grandma Got Run Over by a Reindeer* isn't available, any song performed by singing chipmunks or other woodland creatures that probably taste a whole lot better than they sing works well, too.

*　　　*　　　*

Of course, with every Christmas season comes the controversial "Merry Christmas" versus "Happy Holidays" greeting debate. It seems everybody has an opinion about what is and isn't appropriate to say. These days, I have friends with Christian backgrounds who are too afraid to wish me anything but "Happy Holidays." Other friends with Jewish and Islamic backgrounds wouldn't think twice about wishing me a "Merry Christmas."

As a Christian, I celebrate Christmas, which is the recognized birth date of Jesus Christ, Who I believe died for my sins, rose from the grave, and Who I'm proud to call my Lord and Savior. I realize not everyone celebrates Christmas because different people have different religious views. Though I may not always share the same beliefs as others, I do believe that everyone has the right to make their own choices about the role of religion and spirituality in their lives, or the lack thereof.

This, however, still leaves the question of whether or not it's more appropriate to wish someone "Merry Christmas" or "Happy Holidays." Here's my take on the issue: First, I don't believe the phrase "Happy Holidays" is sacrilegious. Before Thanksgiving, I usually say "Happy Holidays," since I think that covers both Thanksgiving and Christmas. After Thanksgiving, however, I do believe you should wish people a "Merry Christmas." Even if they don't celebrate Christmas, I still want them to have a "Merry Christmas."

When working in the store during this time of year, I found myself on the frontline of the "Merry Christmas/ Happy Holidays" battle. The management encouraged us to wish customers a "Merry Christmas" and I believe in saying it. However, believing in saying something and actually saying it are two different things. In our attempt not to offend anyone, we can unknowingly be preconditioned to be politically correct.

At the start of the Christmas season, I decided to wish customers "Happy Holidays." I figured wishing someone "Happy Holidays" would be the easiest thing to do, and sure enough, I was right. I never had any customer complain that I wished them "Happy Holidays."

Several weeks later, I ran into a wonderful Christian couple that frequently shopped in the store. They knew I was a Christian, and as we talked about the Christmas season, the wife said to me in a loving but matter of fact way, that because of our faith, we both knew what the true meaning of Christmas was all about. I quickly, though quietly, agreed.

We said our goodbyes and she and her husband left. At that moment, I realized wishing someone "Happy Holidays" wasn't enough for me any longer. I knew I had to be doing more. How can someone who calls himself a Christian be embarrassed to wish people a simple "Merry Christmas"?

It was time for action. With just a couple of weeks left in the Christmas season, I began my own personal "Merry Christmas" campaign. Had I waited any longer we would have been celebrating Arbor Day.

I'm ashamed to admit the words, "Merry Christmas," didn't come easy to say at first. At times I felt uncomfortable saying it. With every customer I wished a "Merry Christmas," I never knew what response I would get, and I'll admit it made me a little nervous.

What I quickly learned, however, was that most customers responded by sincerely and enthusiastically wishing me a "Merry Christmas" right back. On some occasions, wishing them a "Merry Christmas" not only seemed to make them happier, but I think some people were shocked that someone (especially someone who works in a retail store) actually had the courage to wish them a

"Merry Christmas." Had I not shown a little courage, I never would have realized this.

I know that for some people, Christmas Day is just another day out of the year, and I respect every person's decision whether or not they choose to celebrate Christmas. To those same people, however, please respect that for many of us, Christmas Day is far more than just another day out of the year. We don't want to be told what we can and cannot say in regard to Christmas. To sum it up, if you insist on trying to take Christ out of Christmas, then don't be surprised if the rest of us retaliate by launching a campaign to take global warming out of Earth Day, and we'll see how you like it.

*   *   *

Recently at work, I had the opportunity to promote one of my all-time favorite products: M&M Cookies. M&M's are tasty little candies, and cookies are great in themselves, but put M&M's in a cookie and you have one of the greatest desserts in the history of modern civilization.

For this particular promotion, I opened individual packs of the M&M Cookies, placed folded napkins on a plate, and proceeded to put one cookie on each napkin for the customers to sample. Needless to say, anybody passing out free cookies becomes very popular very quickly. (Had I given out free cookies in high school, perhaps this would have increased my odds of getting invited to more parties, or perhaps at least one party.)

As boxes of the cookies sold throughout the day, I continued giving away free samples. At one point, I noticed one of the cookies I had poured into my serving bowl was partially broken.

Instead of throwing the broken cookie away, I decided to serve it to the customers anyway. Aside from being partially crumbled on one side, it was still a perfectly good cookie. It had the same great taste as all the other cookies, and I was certain it wouldn't be long until a customer decided to take the broken cookie.

Instead, the customers who came to my cart kept choosing to take the samples of the cookies that were not broken. Everyone left the broken cookie sitting on the plate all by its lonesome on a neatly folded white napkin. At one point, a little boy came to my cart with his parents. I figured he would be so happy to get a free cookie, he would be the one to choose to take the broken cookie. To make sure this happened, the only cookie I left on the plate at the time was the broken cookie. When all the little boy saw was the broken cookie, however, even he decided that he didn't want to take it. It wasn't until I put other cookies on the plate that were not broken that he chose to take one.

Time passed, and I kept waiting for just one customer to realize that the broken cookie was just as delicious as all the other cookies, but still, no one wanted to take the cookie. Eventually it was time for my break. I wheeled my cart to the back of the store with the broken cookie left alone on the plate once again. I left my cart, and a few minutes later I came back to discover that someone, presumably a hungry coworker since customers aren't allowed in the back of the store, finally had seen the cookie for the tasty little snack that it was and decided to eat it.

As I look back on the broken cookie experience, I'm reminded that there are many people in this world that have the same attitude about people as they do about broken cookies. Just as they refuse to eat a broken cookie because they don't think is good enough, they may choose not to associate with people they feel are "broken." Many people have bought into the mistaken beliefs that only the most attractive people who drive the nicest cars, live in the nicest homes, or have the biggest bank accounts are the ones who should get the best treatment. Those that don't fit into this category are often ignored, just like the broken cookie sitting by itself on the plate.

As someone who is physically disabled, I know what it's like to feel like that broken cookie myself. Throughout my life, I've been passed over to make room for those who were deemed to be more socially acceptable. This hurts more than I can begin to describe.

It is for such reasons why the time I spend in my church has become so special to me. The members of my church love and accept me for who I am, and most everyone there views me as important and equal to everyone else.

You'll notice I said *most* everyone. Sadly, there is no such thing as the perfect church, even my own that I love dearly. The truth is, all church members, just like all non-church members, are imperfect themselves. I've heard more than a few stories about unpleasant experiences others have had in certain churches, which ranged from feeling the members of those churches were unkind to them because they were a single parent who had been divorced or because they didn't drive the right kind of car of live in the best neighborhood. I've even heard stories about people that wanted to volunteer their time to work in the church, but were told that there was simply no place for them to serve.

The worst story I ever heard was about a young woman who, on her first Sunday visiting the church, was told in which pews she could and couldn't sit. Certain pews had been designated for church members who made greater financial contributions to the church. She also found out that if she wanted to join the church choir, it was by audition ONLY.

To be fair to those churches, I learned long ago that there are two sides to every story. Some people are denied opportunities to serve in churches for very serious reasons that have nothing to do with where they live or what they drive. As far as choirs auditioning for only the best singers, I can tell you that my sister, Patti, who is our church choir director, has endured some rather painful choir rehearsals through the years, and I'm certain there are times she wishes she had established an "Audition Only" format herself. Patti has also likely wished that just like "No Fly" lists have been created to keep suspected terrorists from getting on airplanes, she wishes church choir directors could come together to create a country-wide "No Sing" list to keep known bad singers out of choirs. Singing loudly and off pitch is considered an act of domestic terrorism by many choir directors.

I'm sure there is some truth to many of the church horror stories I've heard. I know that certain members of my church joined the church because of the negative ways they were treated in other churches. They felt a sense of love and purpose in my church that they didn't feel elsewhere. Through their influence, they have made my church a greater place for me to grow in my faith. Those other churches really missed out on having some great members.

Whenever I think about the issue of favoritism within the church, I'm reminded of one of my favorite books of the Bible, the Book of James. You don't have to be a theology major to understand James. It's written in a way where most verses are easy to understand.

In the second chapter of James (NIV), the issue of favoritism in the church is addressed with the following example: Two men walk into a church service. One man is rich and wearing fine clothes and a gold ring. The other is poor, has no ring, and wears shabby clothes. Both men are greeted by members of the church and are told where to sit. The rich man is given a good seat. The poor man, however, is told he can either remain standing or he can sit on the floor next to the feet of the rich church members.

Now, I'm not rich, and I wouldn't take too kindly to visiting a church and being told I could only sit on the floor next to the feet of everyone else. I would probably stay for the service since I don't believe you should allow man's wrongdoing to come between you and your relationship with God. As I'm sitting there, however, I would be praying that the first hymn they sing has a considerable number of stanzas because while everyone is standing and singing, I would be tying as many shoelaces together as quietly as possible so I wouldn't be noticed. Then, later on during the meet and greet portion of the service where everyone stands up to walk around and meet new people, as they're falling over one another, they would think twice before they asked anybody to sit at their feet ever again.

What we must realize is that God looks down on favoritism. He loves everyone equally, both the rich and the poor. He has given everyone unique gifts and talents, most of which don't require access to a large bank account or stock portfolio to make use of them, either. All that's needed is a simple willingness to obey God.

People that have had a bad experience in church shouldn't

let that experience keep them out of church. They should keep searching until they find a good church where its members show kindness and respect to everyone who walks through the front door, regardless of the condition of their clothes or their car. The best church members know what's most important is the condition of the person's heart, and how God is working inside that heart. That includes us "broken cookies," too.

*   *   *

I have attended the same Baptist church in my hometown of Jacksonville North Carolina, for most of my life. I've seen many wonderful things occur in the church and have also experienced firsthand many of the struggles the church has gone through that helped make it what it is today.

I don't believe the role of the church has changed much through the years, but the perception of the church in today's culture has drastically changed. Many people, including long-time church members, have abandoned the church and its teachings. Some have even bought into the belief that a life without God and the teachings of the church is the most fulfilling life possible. This mindset has hurt the church at a time when it's needed more than ever. When I reflect on the role of the church today and in years to come, I ask myself what the church needs to do not only to survive, but to thrive. I have reached the following conclusions:

First and foremost, churches need strong leadership at every level within the church, starting with the pastor. Pastors come in all shapes and sizes and impact the lives of the people they serve in unique ways. The best pastors show kindness and love to their churches and communities by actively practicing all week long the same Biblical principles they preach from behind the pulpit.

While I'm on the subject of the role of a pastor, I feel that I should share my views on the role of women in church ministry. This can be a touchy subject with some people, and as I'm writing this I'm wondering who will be the first person to offer to drive me to my tar and feathering.

I personally believe that women have the ability and the right to serve in the church as committee members, Sunday school teachers, deacons, and even as pastors, if God is leading them in that direction. God has given women unique opportunities for service that men will never have, nor were they meant to have.

I say to all those faithful women, continue to serve God to the best of your ability. Don't let anyone discourage you, but do allow the people that God has placed in your life to guide and encourage you and even point you back in the right direction if you get off course. These same principles hold true for men as well.

While we're on the subject, I also don't believe that a pastor has to be married to be effective, either. I'm certain there are single pastors who do an outstanding job in their chosen profession. I do believe, though, that a pastor with a supportive spouse can have more opportunities for outreach available than a single pastor has, and may even give a better impression than a single pastor can give.

Let's take the preacher's wardrobe for example.

Through the years, my church has employed both married and single pastors. I think the married pastors looked and dressed nicer. This is likely because they were blessed with a spouse that helped them discern what is and isn't appropriate attire for a church service. I think this is more of a problem with the male pastors since most women I know seem to have a far better fashion sense than many of their male counterparts.

Say, for example, a pastor is getting dressed on Sunday morning. If his wife notices that what he is planning to wear behind the pulpit is likely to frighten the widows or anyone else in the congregation who suffers from chronic heart problems, she can lovingly take him aside, take him by the hand, and calmly inform him that he has exactly five minutes to change out of his outfit or she's going to kill him.

Single pastors aren't as fortunate.

At this time, the pastor of my church is single. As a church body, we've come to the realization that we need to pray that God will bring a woman into his life to give him some pointers on fashion do's and don'ts. This is a man who may have helped coin the term "wardrobe malfunction" long before Janet Jackson ever made it popular. His decision to preach one Sunday morning while wearing a green sports jacket with burgundy pants is now a part of church folklore.

Here's a tip for any single pastor when it comes to picking out your wardrobe: never wear anything that makes you look like you've just come off the PGA tour. It should be noted, though, that if Tiger Woods had worn some of the outfits as my preacher, he might not have encountered as many problems as he has because many of the women he's encountered would have run away screaming.

Wardrobe aside, my minister has many wonderful qualities. He preaches convicting yet uplifting sermons in a clear and concise manner (meaning we know what he's saying word for word and we know we'll be getting out of church in time to beat the Presbyterians to the drive-thru at Wendy's). He also takes an active role in working with various committees within the church and in the community by working with a local crisis pregnancy center. He has reminded us that all human life, from the oldest senior citizen to the smallest unborn baby should be valued equally, and for this, I'm grateful.

*　　　　*　　　　*

In addition to the role of the pastor, the members of a church have important roles to play as well, and they must show wisdom in those roles. If not, minor issues can quickly turn into conflicts that threaten to divide or even destroy the church.

I have seen conflicts arise within the church over the silliest issues. I wouldn't be surprised to learn that somewhere there is a church where one family in the church forgot to send another family in the church a Christmas card during the holidays, which led to the families of the church taking sides. Eventually, the police were called to the church's Christmas pageant after a fist fight broke out between Mary and Joseph and the shepherds began hitting each other with their rods. Baby Jesus probably covered his face in the swaddling cloths out of embarrassment.

My church is no stranger to conflict, either. Through the years I've seen many former church members whom I once respected act in ways that were very disappointing. I won't mention them by name or what they did, though. When you still reside in your hometown, people know exactly where you live and can easily track you down. I will, however, share what I believe are the best ways to avoid conflict within the church.

For starters, I believe long-time members should strive for unity in the church by showing their newer members and visitors alike that they are sincerely loved by God and them as well (with emphasis on the word *sincerely*). This makes it much easier to attract newcomers to the church.

Church members must be careful, though. Even though most people who join churches do so because they seek to deepen their relationship with God, others may join for reasons that are not always the most sincere. They may have hidden agendas that may end up hurting the church and its reputation. Of course, we have to be careful not to judge one another, but as a wise pastor once implied, we should be "fruit inspectors" and make sure the "fruits" of each other's labor is pleasing to God. With God's help, people can change for the better, but they have to want to change first. Some people have no desire to change.

A church should never discriminate against anyone on the basis of income, race, or gender, but I do think more churches should practice "spiritual profiling." If someone wants to join a church and it's discovered they have a history of causing problems in other churches, perhaps that person should not be allowed to join the church at that time. If the leaders of that church believe that individual is sincerely interested in growing in their faith, perhaps then that person should be allowed to join, but only under certain conditions, such as mandatory attendance in the church's *Basics of Christianity* Class or anger management course, *The Sanctuary was Painted Purple Against My Wishes...Now What?* I also think long-time church members who have gotten off track should be treated the same way.

Another way to avoid conflict in the church is to make sure the business of the church is handled properly. In many churches, the members vote on church matters at business meetings. I don't believe, however, that every member of a church should be allowed to vote, especially children. Some churches have no age limit on who has a vote in church matters. In theory, a toddler could vote on who becomes a deacon or even the next pastor. They may even cast the deciding vote. There are reasons why we have age limits for voting in state and national elections – because those who vote must be old enough to have the level of maturity needed to make sound voting choices. In short, an adult who is brought into a church business meeting in a wheel chair should be allowed to vote. A child who is brought into the same meeting in a stroller and has to have a pacifier put in their mouth to keep them quiet during the meeting should **not** be allowed to vote.

The more I think about it, though, perhaps making the most obnoxious loud-mouths in the church (or anywhere else, for that matter) suck on a pacifier to keep them quiet is a good idea, too. If an adult insists on acting like a baby because he or she doesn't get their way, I say treat 'em like a baby and jam that binky up their pie hole until that person learns to act their age. I think this same approach would work quite well at company board meetings as well, along with the previously-mentioned idea of a company-sponsored nap time.

One of the simplest ways to avoid conflict in the church is to keep the lines of communication open between church members. Sadly, I've learned from first-hand experience that some church members act like they're better than everyone else and will only talk to certain people when the mood strikes them, even while in church. Sometimes they are silent for so long that people begin to believe the rumors that those people were kicked in the neck by livestock as children which caused permanent damage to their vocal chords. When they finally do speak, what they say can be so mean and hurtful that everyone would have been better off had they just kept quiet. What incentive do newcomers in the church have to stay there if the long-time members act like they don't want them there in the first place?

It's just as important for church members to work together within the various ministries of the church. While it's true that sometimes people may have to wait to work in certain capacities in the church, this may be because God wants them to learn the importance of patience and humility. I, however, also believe there comes a time when those faithful church members who have held certain positions for many years should step aside and give others the opportunity to serve. They won't be around forever, and when it comes time to fill that vacant position, the church will need people with the experience. They should be willing to allow others to help them so others can learn from their experience.

These are all great ways to avoid conflict in the church, but sometimes no matter how hard everyone tries, conflicts still arise. People still get upset and leave the church for very petty reasons and may even try to get other church members to leave with them. Even in Biblical times, there was division in the church. In the Church of Corinth, some church members chose to follow Paul and others chose to follow Apollos. These days they might say, "I follow Rev. Smith" or "I follow my youth pastor." Some church members even feel they should be the leaders in the church themselves. They believe that if others in the church aren't following them, the church isn't heading in the right direction. What they need to be doing, however, is asking themselves if they're upset because God's plans for the church aren't being accomplished or because their plans aren't being accomplished. Until everyone in the church follows the Jesus group, there will always be conflict.

God doesn't expect perfection from church members, because as long as we're living on this Earth, we'll never achieve perfection. What God does expect is for the church, HIS church, to turn to Him for guidance. God has a plan for all of our lives. One of the best ways to discover that plan is to get involved, and stay involved, in a good Bible-teaching, Bible-preaching, Bible-believing church. It doesn't matter how many members a church has if they aren't willing to attend and work in the church, and just as important, to remain in the church.

I'll conclude this section by sharing a story about an elderly woman in my own church who faithfully taught Sunday school for over thirty years. On the Sunday after her husband of many years had passed away, she was back at church, much to the amazement of other church members who assumed she would be at home grieving over his death. When asked by another church member why she chose to come to church, she informed the well-meaning church member that her husband was the one who had died, NOT her. Perhaps if more people today would learn from the example of this faithful woman, we could return to a time in our culture when people are more upset about missing church than they are about missing out on yet another Sunday morning soccer tournament.

*　　　　*　　　　*

My relationship with God is very special to me, and

when I'm at work, I want those around me to know this. But since I work in a retail setting, I probably won't get a chance to lead a Bible study or prayer group for coworkers. If I were given permission to pass out religious pamphlets to customers, many of them would probably give them back to me once they realized it wasn't a "two-for-one" coupon. There are ways, however, that a person can demonstrate God's love in the workplace. Even if someone has no religious background whatsoever, this is still good advice.

Let's use my job at the store as an example. I've learned that one of the best ways to show God's love to those around me is by showing them respect, and this includes managers and supervisors. Though it's not always easy to do, I show them respect by doing my job to the best of my ability and obeying their authority. I show respect in the way I speak to them, and when they're not around, in the way I speak about them. When I do something wrong (which seldom happens, just in case any of my bosses are reading this), I listen to their constructive criticism, because after taking the time to get to know them, I realize they want me to succeed in my job. When I succeed, it's more likely that the store will succeed.

Showing respect to coworkers is just as important. My coworkers and I come from different backgrounds and work in different departments of the store, but when we put on our name badges with the official store logo, we're all a part of the same team.

One of the best ways to show respect for coworkers is to humble yourself. When I worked with my fellow professional gummy bear giver outers, it wasn't uncommon for us to boast about our daily sales figures, but in time, I leaned to keep it in perspective.

Say, if on the day before Thanksgiving, a fellow gummy bear giver outer proudly announces that as a result of all the roasted turkey samples she passed out, over two-hundred frozen turkeys were sold. Of course, that coworker should be praised for their hard work. Let's face reality, though. We're talking about the day before Thanksgiving here. It's safe to assume most of those frozen turkeys would have sold that day regardless of who was promoting it. Had this person successfully sold two-hundred boxes of chocolate-covered Easter eggs on the day before Thanksgiving, THAT would have justified a little self-glorification.

If you want to be noticed at work, don't be the person who spends your time bragging about how great you are. Instead, be the person who brags about how great your coworkers are, or could be, by taking the time to show them some kindness and encouragement.

One of the best ways to show respect to your coworkers is to treat everyone equally, regardless of what job they do. In the eyes of God, no one person is better than the other. I must confess, though, I have always had a special place in my heart for my store's maintenance crew. They have some of the dirtiest and most thankless jobs in our culture, and they seldom get the thanks they deserve. These wonderful people often perform tasks that no one else wants to do, like having to unclog sinks or being the first responder on the scene of an overflowing toilet. When dealing with the overflowing toilets, not only do they have to use rubber gloves to protect themselves, but in some severe instances they may have to put on diving gear and embark on an underwater expedition that even Jacques Cousteau would have been too afraid to undertake.

I've also learned the importance of showing respect

to the customers or clients we serve in our jobs, which can be challenging. Whenever I find myself dealing with "the other one percent," I remind myself that I may be the only Christian that person meets that day. I need to show them courtesy and respect, regardless of whether I get any in return. Striking up a friendly conversation and getting to know others has the potential to turn even the rudest customers into people you discover you have a lot in common with and look forward to seeing again and again.

When we strive to be the best worker possible, we not only learn to respect others, but also ourselves. We may not always have the job we want, but it may be the job that God wants us to have for reasons that will become clearer as we continue to serve God by serving the people that He has placed in our lives.

*   *   *

Recently, I was given the opportunity to speak before a group of my coworkers during a weekly employee meeting. The topic of the meeting was diversity in the workplace, and my general manager had asked me to speak about what it has been like for me to cope with a disability. I was honored to have been asked to speak, and I gladly accepted the invitation. Besides, I felt sorry for my manager. As anybody who has ever heard me speak in public will tell you, anyone who does ask me to speak is usually pretty desperate for a speaker.

On the day of the meeting, I arrived at work at 8:00 a.m. This time in the morning is usually quiet, and customers are few and far between. I made my way to the training room where the meeting was to take place. Soon coworkers from various departments in the store began filing in one at a time. At one point, I looked around and realized it was now standing room only. Of course, when I considered this was a small room with only twelve chairs and there were fifteen people in the room with only three standing, it helped put it in perspective.

The meeting began with the general manager welcoming us and discussing the weekly sales figures. He then explained the purpose of the meeting that morning was to raise awareness of diversity in the workplace and that I would be speaking momentarily. The first guest speaker of the morning was a wonderful lady named Kim, who for the last several years has been my advocate and counselor with North Carolina Division of Services for the Blind. Kim spoke about what services her organization offered people like me who are visually impaired. Many people in the crowd found her talk interesting because not everybody, including myself for many years, realized what services and agencies are available to help those that are disabled live a better life.

Following Kim's talk, the general manger introduced me, though I had worked there long enough that introductions weren't necessary. I began by letting everyone know I was glad to be speaking and asked them to be patient with me because I wasn't used to speaking to crowds so early in the morning. I usually didn't arrive at work until 11 a.m. and wasn't usually even fully awake until 3 p.m. I told everyone I would try to keep my talk brief. (Their reaction was similar to when a preacher says he'll be brief, so it was good to know there were potentially regular churchgoers in the crowd.) I let them know that if I began to ramble on, they should wave their arms in the air to get my attention.

If they used their fingers to point to their watches, it would only remind me that I was on the clock and being paid to speak that morning, and the longer I spoke, the more I was paid.

I told the crowd that I would be talking about how being legally blind had affected me throughout my life. I wanted to get as specific as possible because many people tend to place groups like the disabled into the same negative category. They falsely assume that disabled individuals will never accomplish anything worthwhile. I wanted to remind the group that every person, including someone with a disability, is unique and has a unique story to tell.

I gave a brief description of my specific visual impairments, starting with Congenital Optic Atrophy, which caused the optic nerves in my eyes to never fully develop, along with Nystagmus, which makes it harder to focus on the same objects for long periods of time because my eyes move rapidly. To put it in perspective, let's say I'm out on a date in a restaurant. As I'm talking to my date, an attractive waitress walks by and my eyes move quickly away from my date and towards the waitress. If my date angrily says to me, "Were you staring at that waitress?" I could truthfully say "It's likely I was, but it's beyond my control." (This may be why I get even fewer second dates than I do speaking engagements.)

Next, I explained how being legally blind affected me when I was back in school. Despite my disability, I was a pretty good student and many subjects came easy to me. Mathematics, however, was a different story. Add severe eye strain to the equation and it made a bad situation worse. I often sat in class and stared at the math problems on my paper, unable to come up with the answers. The longer I stared, the more blurry the numbers grew, and sometimes I saw numbers that weren't even there. The number 237 might begin to look like 3,877. I told everyone if there was anything good about having this problem is that when I looked at my paycheck and thought it was too small, if I stared at the amount long enough, it would grow larger before my eyes. An amount of $237 would eventually look like $3,877. The only downside was finding a bank teller who suffered from the same visual impairment when it came time to cash the check.

I went on to mention that one of the biggest differences between me and my classmates was that because I was so nearsighted, I always sat in the front of the classroom so I could see the blackboard. Since there is seldom a rush among children to sit in the front of the class, I never had any real trouble finding a seat.

I'm convinced that sitting in the front of the classroom made me a better student, though. I could see the board well enough to take good notes in class and was much closer to where the teacher was standing. This made it harder to get into as much trouble as my classmates who sat in the back of the class using their time to pass notes and draw pictures of the teacher that made that teacher look like the star attraction at Sea World.

Sitting in the front of the classroom never really bothered me until college. I often found myself sitting in considerably larger classrooms with seating for well over thirty to forty students per class. If, say, there were only fifteen students in the class, I usually ended up alone up front with fourteen of my classmates fighting for the seats in the back row. Being alone up front with just the teacher to keep me company was sometimes quite depressing.

I will admit, though, whenever a nasty stomach virus was going around campus and all of my classmates who sat close to one another in the back were dropping like flies, whenever they returned to class and were desperate to borrow my class notes, it was all I could do at times to keep the smile off my face.

The classroom illustration helped transition me to how coping with a disability affected my social life. I told everyone that I never had one specific traumatic experience related to my disability, but one bad day that stuck out in my mind was my sixteenth birthday. I knew I couldn't see well enough to get a driver's license, which is perhaps the greatest rite of passage for any teenager. Many teenagers believe if you can't drive to a party you shouldn't be invited to one. As a result of this mindset, I spent many nights alone back in high school.

Since I didn't drive, my father drove me to school. I love my father and I'm grateful he was willing to drive me, but sometimes it was embarrassing. Once I even had a classmate who had the nerve to make fun of my father's car, which at the time was a 1987 Dodge Colt Vista Wagon.

Anyone that has ever belittled the '87 Vista Wagon has obviously never had the privilege of riding in one. It wasn't what many would consider to be the most stylish vehicle, but the Vista Wagon had the best headroom of any vehicle we've ever owned and had seating for six. When you needed to carry large objects in the car, you could fold down the two rows of backseats which provided more than enough space to carry a large office chair or washing machine. It was worth keeping the car for all the money we saved on delivery costs alone. Eventually, my father sold the car when the air-conditioning stopped working and we were having trouble starting the car in the morning. Any time you have to use an electric power drill to turn the ignition switch, it's time to trade.

Had I gotten a driver's license, I would have been proud to drive the Vista Wagon. Nobody should ever make fun of somebody else's vehicle. Besides, try carrying a washing machine in the back of a Mustang or Camaro and you'll quickly change your tune.

The next part of my speech was on what having a disability meant to me as an employee at the store. I talked about how grateful I was to be working there, but looking back, I realize I didn't talk as much about working in the store as I should have. So many people show little, if any, interest in their jobs because they believe their job is "beneath them." Then there are others who want to work, like the disabled, who are denied opportunities for employment, even though they're willing to work just as hard, if not harder, than those who are not disabled.

It reminds me of the time my parents and I were traveling through central Illinois on our way to visit an aunt in St. Louis. We decided to pull over at a rural rest stop for a few minutes. As my father and I walked into the men's restroom, we encountered a group of young men in their late teens or early twenties cleaning the floors and toilets. We quickly realized they all suffered from some type of disability, presumably Down syndrome or something similar. At first I felt sorry for these young men. But as I began to look around the restroom and saw just how clean it was, I realized these young men took as much pride, if not more pride, in their jobs than many people who didn't suffer from a disability. There are many people who see the disabled doing jobs that they themselves would never consider doing in a million years and feel sorry for them. I also believe many disabled people actually feel sorry for these people because many disabled workers will go the extra mile to be the best worker they can be, even if that means taking the jobs no one else wants to do.

I concluded my talk by sharing with everyone what the Bible says about teamwork. I wanted to do this in a way that everyone there could relate to it, regardless of their religious backgrounds. I spoke of the verses in I Corinthians where the body of the church is compared to different parts of the human body and how all the separate parts must work together for the greater good of the church. To put this in perspective, those that God made the "ears" are great at hearing about the needs of those around them and can best determine how to help them. The "eyes" see what needs to be done. The "feet" travel to where the needs are, and the "hands" help meet those needs. Of course, in some churches you have that small group of people that are the "butts," but there's never quite enough time to discuss them as I would like.

I compared the Biblical view of teamwork to our jobs at the store. The "ears" were the employees who listened to the questions of our customers and addressed their concerns. The "eyes" were responsible for seeing when the shelves needed to be restocked and spills needed to be cleaned up. The "feet" went to where the customers or potential customers were to tell them what our store had to offer them. The "hands" stocked the shelves, cleaned the spills, changed tires in the automotive department, manned the cash registers, and loaded heavy boxes into the customers' cars.

As a product demonstrator, I was the "mouth." I told

customers about various products, some of which they had never heard of or tasted before they had met me. I was able to sell them products that hopefully they liked enough to keep buying in our store for years to come.

I concluded my speech and thanked everyone for listening. I can't say for sure if anybody who heard me speak that day benefited from what I said, but I know I did. By reminding others what the Bible says about teamwork, I reminded myself that no matter who we are or what we do, when we work with others, we must be willing to work together as a team. This includes letting others that are different from us, including the disabled, be a part of that same team. A person may not always be able to be the "hands," "feet," or "eyes," of the team, but if they have the desire to do the best they can and encourage others to do the same, they will quickly become "the heart" of the team.

Chapter 6

The Professional Gummy Bear Giver Outer's Last Stand

IT'S BEEN SAID THAT ALL good things must come to an end. This saying holds true for good books, good meals, and sadly, even good jobs.

It started on a Friday afternoon. I was off from work and received a telephone call from my departmental manager. He told me to be at the store on Sunday morning at 8 a.m. for a mandatory meeting. Everyone in my department was to be in attendance. Since the meeting was to begin two hours before our usual Sunday shift started, I grew curious as to what we would be discussing. When I asked my manager, he wasn't able (or wasn't willing) to give me a definite answer. This did nothing to assure me that everything was going to be fine.

On Saturday, I was back at work. By now, the rumors of what would take place at Sunday's meeting were being discussed openly (albeit quietly) among the professional gummy bear giver outers. We tried to reassure one another there was nothing to worry about, but reassurance without any facts to support it goes only so far. Later that evening, as I lay in bed, I knew in my heart that something big was about to happen. In only a matter of hours, the truth would be revealed, and we would learn if all our worry was in vain, or in fact, was quite justifiable.

On Sunday morning, shortly before 8 a.m., my coworkers and I began arriving at work. We all sat together in the café in the front of the store. After everyone had finally arrived, we were instructed by our manager to follow him. He spoke few words as he led us to the back of the store. As we walked together, we wondered if this would indeed be the final "march of the penguins."

At the time of the meeting, the store was several months into a major renovation project. We discovered our meeting was to take place in a part of the sales floor that weeks earlier had been filled with steel shelves crammed with merchandise. By now it was just a wide open area of concrete. Through the years, the professional gummy bear giver outers had been responsible for promoting various items in this part of the store, such as dog food, cat litter, and household cleaning supplies. These items were some of the most difficult ones to sell, partly because there never seemed to be quite as much foot traffic in this area. Because of this, this part of the sales floor had long ago been dubbed, rather ironically, as the "dead zone." Mysterious meetings held in places known as the "dead zone" seldom calm the nerves of anxious store employees.

What was different about the "dead zone" on this morning was that the area was filled with pallets on the floor stacked with packages of paper towels and bottled water. We made our way to the other side of the pallets and were greeted by three neat rows of folding chairs. A few yards from the chairs were three small tables, several yards away from each table. Each table had two chairs, one on either side of the table. Our general manager stood near the tables and near him stood several managers of various departments. Everyone was eerily quiet.

After everyone sat down, I began looking at the pallets filled with merchandise. When sitting in the chairs, we were unable to see over them. It was as if a makeshift wall had been constructed to keep outsiders from seeing what we would be taking place within the next few moments.

We remained seated and waited for the meeting to begin. It seemed as if we had already been sitting there for all of eternity. I know we've all heard that saying one too many times, but any worker who has ever faced this situation can tell you, it truly does feel like an eternity.

The general manager continued to stand up front, looking at us in total silence. He had only been at our store for a few months and nobody was sure exactly what he would say. When he finally spoke, the first thing he said was that he had some difficult news. These aren't the words any employee ever wants to ever hear from their boss. Most employees know that after their boss tells them he has difficult news, the next words they hear are not likely going to be, "I hate to tell you this, but your bonuses this year will be so large that it will put you in a higher tax bracket."

The general manager continued speaking. He informed us that the decision had been made by our company to outsource our department to a third-party company that would come in to take over our duties. Effective immediately, the professional gummy bear giver outers of the store were no more. We were being replaced with professional gummy bear giver outer outsiders.

We learned that the new company coming in would be hiring people to do our old jobs and anyone interested in continuing to work as a product demonstrator was eligible to apply, which I suppose would make them professional gummy bear giver outer outsider insiders. We were also given the option to apply for other current job openings in the store and new positions that would become available after the renovation project was completed later that year. We were given more options than many workers are ever given. Even so, there were still many tears cried that Sunday morning.

Over the next few days, several coworkers and I were able to secure other jobs within the store. I accepted a position as a part-time sales clerk in the Electronics Department. On my first day back at work, as I made my way to the back of the store to clock in for my shift, I walked through what was left of my former department. By now, my former supervisor's desk had already been removed, and our serving carts, which for years had been used to stack merchandise on top for customers to purchase, were now stacked on top of each other and wheeled into our former kitchen to be stored indefinitely. A department that had functioned for so many years had now ceased to exist. The following evening, as I lay in bed, I realized just how much my former job had really meant to me. It was my turn to cry my own tears for the professional gummy bear giver outers. I guess the old saying is right, and that you truly don't know what you've got until it's gone.

I knew I couldn't dwell on the past. I had a new job waiting for me in Electronics, and with this new job came many new responsibilities. I was now responsible for speaking to the customers about the merchandise, helping customers locate merchandise, and making sure the electronics were clean at all times. I had gone from being a professional gummy bear giver outer to becoming a professional television duster. When the boss wasn't around, though, sometimes I became a professional television watcher.

When I began training for my new job, I had to learn a lot about electronics in a very short period of time. When it came to learning about computers, I'll admit that even to this day, I still have trouble figuring out which wire goes where. When people ask me what's the difference between two laptops, they're usually not impressed when I look down at both computers, look up, and say, "Well, this one here is black, and the other one is blue. Did I answer your question?" Another thing about computers I still find confusing is the concept of computer memory, especially since computers seem to have better memories than most people. I'm also still trying to learn what a gigabyte is. Like many terms, it sounds like yet another medical ailment (e.g. Poor Aunt Gladys. Just when she had the chronic Wikipedia under control and the body mist finally went away, she was rushed to the dentist with a bad case of gigabyte.)

Thankfully, learning about the differences in television brands came much easier for me, though I'm far from being an expert. One thing I've learned about televisions is that a pixel is something that when combined with other pixels, helps create the images you see on the television screen. Up until then, I had always thought a "pixel" was a fictional creature in an animated Disney film.

Another thing I learned about televisions was that when there are construction workers doing repair work on the roof of the store directly above where the most expensive flat screen televisions are kept, if a hole is cut in the roof and water and insulation are falling directly on top of the televisions while those same televisions are plugged in, it makes for an unsafe work environment. I also learned that when I tried unplugging the televisions, lifting them off the shelf, and transporting them to another location on a flatbed, that made for an even more unsafe work environment.

Though I faced many struggles in my job, I quickly discovered I was blessed with coworkers who were kind enough to come to my rescue. There was always someone there to help me better explain a laptop computer to a customer or help lift a heavy TV box or whatever it was that I needed at that moment. Most of these coworkers didn't even work in my department. They took the time to help me because they cared about me and wanted me to succeed. It was as if the strongest "body parts" had united to help its weakest part. Through their help, the body had been made whole.

*   *   *

In trying to decide how to best conclude this book, I reached for my Bible in the hope that it would provide me with the same divine inspiration that it has given me throughout my writing. After a few moments of flipping through its worn pages, I finally came to the verse in II Thessalonians (NIV) that says, "And as for you, brothers, never tire of doing what is right."

Here's my interpretation: Work hard to get done what needs to get done.

Whether you're working as a professional gummy bear giver outer in a retail store, working the night shift in a restaurant, or volunteering your time to help make your place of worship or community a better place to serve and to live, always remember to rely on God for the strength needed to complete the task at hand. Whatever the job, always strive to be the best worker you can be, because none of us knows for sure when we will "clock out" for the last time.

Thanks for taking the time to read my book. Now, get to work!